AWS Elemental MediaLive User Guide

A catalogue record for this book is available from the Hong Kong Public Libraries.

Published in Hong Kong by Samurai Media Limited.

Email: info@samuraimedia.org

ISBN 9789888408436

Contents

What Is AWS Elemental MediaLive?

AWS Elemental MediaLive is a real-time video service that lets you easily create live outputs for broadcast and streaming delivery.

- Related Services

Related Services

**AWS Identity and Access Management (IAM) ** is a web service that helps you securely control access to AWS resources for your users. Use IAM to control who can use your AWS resources (authentication) and what resources users can use in which ways (authorization). For more information, see [ERROR] BAD/MISSING LINK TEXT

Amazon S3 is storage for the Internet. Use Amazon S3 to store assets that AWS Elemental MediaLive retrieves and uses when transcoding, and as a destination for output from AWS Elemental MediaLive.

Amazon CloudWatch is a monitoring service for AWS Cloud resources and the applications that you run on AWS. Use CloudWatch to track AWS Elemental MediaLive events about the progress of running channels and about metrics such as ingress and egress request count.

AWS Elemental MediaPackage is a just-in-time video packaging and origination service that runs in the AWS Cloud. Use AWS Elemental MediaPackage to package content that has been encoded by AWS Elemental MediaLive.

AWS Elemental MediaStore is a video origination and storage service that offers the high performance and immediate consistency required for live and on-demand media. Use AWS Elemental MediaStore to store assets that AWS Elemental MediaLive retrieves and uses when transcoding, and as a destination for output from AWS Elemental MediaLive.

Setting Up AWS Elemental MediaLive

This chapter provides a basic procedure for setting up identities (users) and providing access to AWS Elemental MediaLive. It describes how to create one or more users as administrators for the service, how to create one or more AWS IAM users to access the AWS Elemental MediaLive console, and how to set up AWS Elemental MediaLive itself as an AWS IAM "trusted service".

If you are completely new to AWS or if you have only been using AWS for a few weeks, we recommend that you read this entire chapter.

If you have more experience using AWS services, you could skip the sections on setting up users. But you must read the section on setting up AWS Elemental MediaLive as a trusted service.

This chapter provides steps for a basic setup. For detailed information on the many features of IAM that may be appropriate and useful to your deployment, see AWS IAM User Guide.

- Required Permissions in AWS Elemental MediaLive
- Sign Up for AWS Elemental MediaLive
- Create an IAM User
- Access to Amazon EC2 Systems Manager Parameter Store
- Access to Amazon S3
- Access to AWS Elemental MediaStore
- Setting up Trusted Entity
- Set up Permissions for AWS Elemental MediaLive

Required Permissions in AWS Elemental MediaLive

There are several identities that must have permissions to work with AWS Elemental MediaLive.

- Any person who is using the console, the CLI, or the REST API (via a REST client application) must have the appropriate permissions on the desired operations of AWS Elemental MediaLive. This access is conferred by setting up people as IAM users.

- Any software application that is using the REST API or an SDK must have the appropriate permissions on the desired operations of AWS Elemental MediaLive. One way to confer this access is by setting up software applications as IAM users.

- AWS Elemental MediaLive itself must be an IAM trusted entity in order to make calls to the APIs of Amazon EC2 Systems Manager Parameter Store, Amazon S3 (if you plan to store and/or retrieve assets on this service) and AWS Elemental MediaStore (if you plan to store and/or retrieve assets on this service). It is extremely likely that AWS Elemental MediaLive will need to be set up in this way.

- The person who sets up AWS Elemental MediaLive as a trusted entity needs read/write access with Amazon IAM. See [ERROR] BAD/MISSING LINK TEXT.

Sign Up for AWS Elemental MediaLive

If you do not have an AWS account, use the following procedure to create one.

To sign up for AWS

1. Open https://aws.amazon.com/ and choose **Create an AWS Account**.

2. Follow the online instructions.

Create an IAM User

To create an IAM user for yourself and add the user to an Administrators group

1. Use your AWS account email address and password to sign in as the *AWS account root user* to the IAM console at https://console.aws.amazon.com/iam/. **Note**
   We strongly recommend that you adhere to the best practice of using the **Administrator** user below and securely lock away the root user credentials. Sign in as the root user only to perform a few account and service management tasks.

2. In the navigation pane of the console, choose **Users**, and then choose **Add user**.

3. For **User name**, type ** Administrator**.

4. Select the check box next to **AWS Management Console access**, select **Custom password**, and then type the new user's password in the text box. You can optionally select **Require password reset** to force the user to select a new password the next time the user signs in.

5. Choose **Next: Permissions**.

6. On the **Set permissions for user** page, choose **Add user to group**.

7. Choose **Create group**.

8. In the **Create group** dialog box, type ** Administrators**.

9. For **Filter**, choose **Job function**.

10. In the policy list, select the check box for ** AdministratorAccess**. Then choose **Create group**.

11. Back in the list of groups, select the check box for your new group. Choose **Refresh** if necessary to see the group in the list.

12. Choose **Next: Review** to see the list of group memberships to be added to the new user. When you are ready to proceed, choose **Create user**.

You can use this same process to create more groups and users, and to give your users access to your AWS account resources. To learn about using policies to restrict users' permissions to specific AWS resources, go to Access Management and Example Policies.

Access to Amazon EC2 Systems Manager Parameter Store

The Amazon EC2 Systems Manager Parameter Store is used extensively in AWS Elemental MediaLive. It is likely that you will use this store. The store holds passwords that the AWS Elemental MediaLive needs in order to retrieve and store files externally.

Some of the features that store passwords in this way are:

- An input of type RTMP Pull or type HLS Pull. The connection to the source is always secure.

- Fields in the channel that hold the URL to an external file, if the connection is secure.Examples of this type of field are the Avail blanking image, and a source captions file that is an external file.

- The destination in an HLS output group or a Micrsoft Smooth output group, if the connection is secure.

In all these cases, if the connection is secure (typically HTTPS), then AWS Elemental MediaLive needs the username and password (stored in a parameter).

How It Works

The password parameter feature ensures that you are not storing passwords in plain text on the console. Instead, you create a password parameter in Amazon EC2 Systems Manager Parameter Store. The parameter is a name/value pair where the name is something like "corporateStorageImagesPassword" and the value is the actual password. When creating a channel or input in AWS Elemental MediaLive, you specify the password parameter name instead of the password. Then when AWS Elemental MediaLive needs the password (in order to either read or write to the external location), it sends the password parameter name to the Amazon EC2 Systems Manager Parameter Store and gets back the actual password in response.

Wherever a password field appears on the console, AWS Elemental MediaLive includes a feature that lets you:

- Specify a password parameter that has already been created in Amazon EC2 Systems Manager Parameter.

- Or create a password parameter "on the spot". You type in a name and the actual password.

Required Permissions

For any user to create a password parameter "on the spot", AWS Elemental MediaLive must have a trusted entity role that includes Amazon EC2 Systems Manager Parameter. See [ERROR] BAD/MISSING LINK TEXT.

Access to Amazon S3

Your deployment may include using files in an Amazon S3 bucket. For example:

- The source for an HLS input.

- The destination for an Archive output group.

- The destination for an HLS output group.

In all these cases, regardless of whether the connection is secure or not, AWS Elemental MediaLive must have a trusted entity role that includes Amazon S3. See [ERROR] BAD/MISSING LINK TEXT.

Access to AWS Elemental MediaStore

Your deployment may include using files in an AWS Elemental MediaStore container. For example:

- The source for an HLS input.
- The destination for an HLS output group.

In all these cases, AWS Elemental MediaLive must have a trusted entity role that includes AWS Elemental MediaStore. See [ERROR] BAD/MISSING LINK TEXT

Setting up Trusted Entity

This permission only needs to be assigned once for all users of the console, CLI, and REST API. There are options for assigning this permission:

- Using the IAM role fields that appear in the General info pane when the first user starts creating the first channel.

  This option is very convenient, but it requires that the console user have read/write access on Amazon IAM, because that user will be sending a request to Amazon IAM to set up AWS Elemental MediaLive as a trusted entity with Amazon EC2 Systems Manager Parameter (and, incidentally, with Amazon S3 and AWS Elemental MediaStore, which are two other services that AWS Elemental MediaLive probably needs to access on your behalf).

  To set up in this way, see [ERROR] BAD/MISSING LINK TEXT. Remember that only one user needs to perform this setup. Subsequent users can choose the existing role.

- By going into IAM and setting up AWS Elemental MediaLive as a trusted entity.

  This option also requires access to Amazon IAM, but typically an administrator who has this access will perform this setup on behalf of all users, before the users start using the console.

  To set up in this way, see [ERROR] BAD/MISSING LINK TEXT.

Both these options result in the creation of a role and a role ARN that is shared by all users (in the AWS account) of the console, CLI, and REST API. The role is called MediaLiveAccessRole and the ARN belongs to that role.

Set up Permissions for AWS Elemental MediaLive

AWS Elemental MediaLive needs permission to make calls to the APIs of Amazon EC2 Systems Manager Parameter Store, Amazon S3 (if you plan to store and/or retrieve assets on this service) and AWS Elemental MediaStore (if you plan to store and/or retrieve assets on this service). You set this permission as follows:

- You create a role called MediaLiveAccessRole and associate one policy with that role.
- You create a second policy that gives access to more services, then associate that policy with the role.
- You modify the trust relationship between your AWS account and the AWS Elemental MediaLive service.

Step 1: Create a Role for the Service

You must create a role for AWS Elemental MediaLive. The role sets up a trusted relationship between your AWS account and AWS Elemental MediaLive.

1. Open the IAM console.

2. In the navigation pane, choose Roles.

3. On the Role page, choose Create role.

4. In the Create role page, in Select type of trusted entity, choose AWS service as the type (the default).

5. In Choose the service that will use this role, choose EC2.

   You are choosing EC2 because AWS Elemental MediaLive is not currently included in this list. Choosing EC2 lets you create a role; in a later step you will change this role to mention AWS Elemental MediaLive instead of EC2.

6. In Select your use case, choose EC2. (Again, you will later change this service to AWS Elemental MediaLive.)

7. Choose Next: Permissions in order to create a policy for this role.

8. Choose AmazonSSMReadOnlyAccess and choose Next: Review.

9. In Role name, type a name. We strongly recommend using the name "MediaLiveAccessRole".

10. Look at the other fields: Amazon EC2 is a trusted entity and the policy attached to this role is AmazonSSMReadOnlyAccess

11. Choose Create role.

Step 2: Modify the Policy

You attached a policy that gives access to AmazonSSMReadOnlyAccess. "SSM" refers to the Amazon EC2 Systems Manager Parameter Store. You must now create a second policy to give access to Amazon S3 and AWS Elemental MediaStore,:

1. From the Role list, choose the role you just created.

2. On Summary, choose Add inline policy.

3. On Set permissions, choose Custom Policy and choose Select.

4. On Review policy, in Policy name, type a suitable name such as S3andMediaStoreReadWriteAccess.

5. In Policy document, paste the following:

```
 1 {
 2    "Version": "2012-10-17",
 3    "Statement": [
 4      {
 5        "Effect": "Allow",
 6        "Action": [
 7          "s3:ListBucket",
 8          "s3:PutObject",
 9          "s3:GetObject",
10          "s3:DeleteObject"
11          ],
12        "Resource": "*"
13      },
14      {
15        "Effect": "Allow",
16        "Action": [
17        "mediastore:ListContainer",
18        "mediastore:DescribeObject",
19        "mediastore:PutObject",
20        "mediastore:GetObject",
21        "mediastore:DeleteObject"
22          ],
23        "Resource": "*"
24      }
25    ]
26 }
```

These lines allow AWS Elemental MediaLive to access Amazon S3 and AWS Elemental MediaStore.

6. Choose Validate Policy, then choose Apply Policy.

7. In the Summary page, you can see that the role MediaLiveAccessRole now has two policies: AmazonSSM-ReadOnlyAccess and S3AndMediaStoreReadWriteAccess. Both policies apply equally to this role.

Step 3: Revise the Trust Relationship

When you created the role and established the trusted relationship, you chose EC2 as the service. You must now modify the role so that the trusted relationship is between your AWS account and AWS Elemental MediaLive.

1. In the Summary page for MediaLiveAccessRole (which should still be displayed), choose Trust relationships.

2. Choose Edit trust relationship.

3. In Edit Trust Relationship, in Policy Document, look at the text that is currently there. It mentions EC2.

4. In Policy Document, paste the following in order to change the policy to mention AWS Elemental MediaLive instead of EC2:

```
 1 {
 2    "Version": "2012-10-17",
 3    "Statement": [
 4      {
 5        "Effect": "Allow",
 6        "Principal": {
 7        "Service": "medialive.amazonaws.com"
 8        },
 9        "Action": "sts:AssumeRole"
```

```
10        }
11    ]
12 }
```

5. Choose Update Trust Policy.

6. On the Summary page, make a note of the value in Role ARN. It looks like this:

   arn:aws:iam::111122223333:role/MediaLiveAccessRole, where 111122223333 is your AWS account number.

   You will use this Role ARN when using AWS Elemental MediaLive, so either make a note of it now, or be prepared to come back to this page to obtain it as required.

Getting Started with AWS Elemental MediaLive

This tutorial describes how to ingest a video source from an RTP source and generate one HLS output that contains one H.264 video encode and one audio encode. AWS Elemental MediaLive will send the output to AWS Elemental MediaPackage. The output will consist of the following:

- One master manifest: channel.m3u8

- One rendition manifest called channel_1.m3u8.

- TS files for each output: channel_1.00001.ts, channel_1.00002.ts, channel_1.00003.ts, and so on.

This tutorial uses the default values for most configuration fields in the channel.

Note
All the text marked as an example in this tutorial is just that – a sample that shows what a piece of information typically looks like. You must replace each example with the information that is valid for your situation.

Prerequisites

Before you can use AWS Elemental MediaLive, you need an AWS account and the appropriate permissions to access, create and view AWS Elemental MediaLive components. Complete the steps in [ERROR] BAD/MISSING LINK TEXT and then return to this tutorial. You will not be able to use AWS Elemental MediaLive, even as an administrator with full access, until you have performed those steps.

Step 1: Set up the Upstream System

The upstream system is the system that is streaming the video to AWS Elemental MediaLive. A contribution encode "on the ground" is a typical upstream system. You must perform some setup of your upstream system before you start working in AWS Elemental MediaLive. For the purposes of this tutorial, the upstream system must be capable of sending a video stream via RTP.

1. Set up your upstream system to perform an RTP push from a specific IP address.

   In a typical deployment of AWS Elemental MediaLive, you provide two sources of the video asset you want to encode. But for this tutorial, you have only one source that you will duplicate within AWS Elemental MediaLive. This setup is absolutely not recommended for production usage.

2. Make a note of the IP address. For example, 192.0.2.0.

3. Keep in mind that the input will need to be ready when you start the associated channel.

Step 2: Set up the Downstream System

In this tutorial, the downstream system (the destination for the output from AWS Elemental MediaLive) is AWS Elemental MediaPackage.

You must set up a channel in this service and you must set it up now because you need the input URLs that AWS Elemental MediaPackage will generate; you enter these input URLs into AWS Elemental MediaLive. You must create two channels in AWS Elemental MediaPackage because you will create two destinations in AWS Elemental MediaLive.

1. Go to the AWS Elemental MediaPackage console.

2. In a new web browser tab or window, display the Getting Started for AWS Elemental MediaPackage and follow steps 1 to 3 to create one channel and its endpoint.

3. Make a note of the input URL, name, and password that AWS Elemental MediaPackage generates. For example:

   - https://39fuo4/.mediapackage/.us/-east/-1/.amazonaws/.com/in/v1/88dpie/channel
   - ue739wuty
   - due484u

   Your channel may be in a different region from the example.

4. Follow steps 1 to 3 again to create the second channel and its endpoint.

5. Make a note of the input URL, name, and password. For example:

   - https://mgu654/.mediapackage/.us/-east/-1/.amazonaws/.com/in/v1/xmm9s/channel
   - 883hdux
   - 634hjik

6. Do not close this web browser yet.

Step 3: Create an Input

You must create an input; this input describes how the source video asset will be provided to AWS Elemental MediaLive. In this tutorial, you will create an RTP input.

You must also create an input security group for the input. This input security group applies the rule "only this specific IP address (an IP address that you own) can push to this input on AWS Elemental MediaLive". Without the protection of this rule, any third party could push content to an AWS Elemental MediaLive input if they knew the IP address and port of the input.

1. Using your IAM credentials, sign in to the AWS Elemental MediaLive console at https://console\.aws\.amazon\.com/medialive?region="region"\.

2. In the navigation pane, choose **Inputs**.

3. On the **Inputs** page, choose **Create input**.

4. In the **Input details** section, for **Input** name, type "My RTP push".

5. For **Input type**, choose **RTP**.

6. In **Input security group**, choose Create new.

7. In **New security group**, type or paste the IP address that you noted in step 1. Enter the address as a CIDR. For example, 192.0.2.0/32.

8. Choose **Create input security group**.

9. Choose **Create** to create the input.

   AWS Elemental MediaLive adds the input to the list of inputs and automatically creates two destinations (one primary and one redundant). These destinations include the port 5000. For example, rtp://198.51.100.0:5000 and rtp://198.51.100.44:5000. These are the two locations where the upstream system must push the source.

10. Make a note of these two addresses: you will need them in step 8.

Step 4: Attach the Input

Now you start creating a channel. The first step in creating a channel is to identify the input . The channel contains the details that instruct AWS Elemental MediaLive how to transcode (decode and encode) and package that input into specific outputs.

1. On the console, choose **Channels** in the navigation pane.

2. In the content pane, choose **Create channel**.

3. In the **Channel and input details** pane, in **General info**, in **Channel Name**, type "Test channel".

4. In **Role ARN**, type the ARN of the role you created when you set up permissions for your AWS account. For example,

   arn:aws:iam::736754895224:role/AllowMediaLiveAccessRole.

5. Select **Remember ARN**.

6. In the **Attach input** section, in **Input**, choose "My RTP push" (the input you created). More fields appear.

7. In **Audio** selectors, choose **Add audio selectors**.

8. In **Audio selector name**, type "My audio source".

   There is no need to complete any other fields on this panel. Specifically:

   - There is no need to create a video selector: when the channel starts, AWS Elemental MediaLive will automatically select the video (or the first video) in the input.

   - In the audio selector, there is no need to specify the PID or language: when the channel starts, AWS Elemental MediaLive will automatically select the first audio, which is acceptable for this tutorial.

   - There is no need to create a captions selector. Typically you will include captions in the channel configuration, but in this tutorial we are omitting them.

Step 5: Create an HLS Output Group

1. In the navigation bar, move down to **Output groups** and choose **Add**.

2. Choose **HLS** and choose **Confirm**.

3. In **Name**, type "MyHLS".

4. In **CDN settings**, choose **Hls webdav**. This is the connection that AWS Elemental MediaPackage (the downstream system for the channel output) uses.

   Leave the defaults for all the other CDN fields.

5. In **HLS group destination A**, in **URL**, type or paste the first input URL that AWS Elemental MediaPackage created for you in step 2. For example, https://39fuo4/.mediapackage/.us/-east/-1/ .amazonaws/.com/in/v1/88dpie/channel/.

6. In **Credentials**, in **Username**, type or paste the username that corresponds to this URL. For example, ue739wuty.

7. In **Password**, choose **Create new parameter**.

8. In **Name**, type "DestinationA_MyHLS".

9. In **Password**, type or paste the password that corresponds to the URL. For example, due484u.

10. Click **Create new parameter**.

    You have created a parameter that holds the password. The parameter is stored in the Amazon EC2 Systems Manager Parameter Store. For more information, see [ERROR] BAD/MISSING LINK TEXT.

11. In **HLS group destination B**, in **URL**, type or paste the second input URL that AWS Elemental MediaPackage created for you in step 2. For example, https://mgu654/.mediapackage/.us/-east/-1/ .amazonaws/.com/in/v1/xmm9s/channel/.

12. In **Credentials**, in **Username**, type or paste the username that corresponds to this URL. For example, 883hdux.

13. In **Password**, choose **Create new parameter**.

14. In **Name**, type "DestinationB_MyHLS".

15. In **Password**, type or paste the password that corresponds to the URL. For example, 634hjik.

16. Click **Create new parameter**.

    You have created a parameter that holds this second password. This parameter is also stored in the Amazon EC2 Systems Manager Parameter Store.

17. Leave the default values in all other fields on this pane.

Step 6: Set up the Output and Encodes

1. In the navigation pane, choose **Output 1**. This output was automatically added when you created the output group. In addition, the output was automatically set up with one video and one audio, as shown in **Stream settings**.

2. In **Stream settings** choose Video.

3. In **Video description name**, change the default name to "H264 video".

   Leave the remaining fields with the default values. Specifically, leave Width and Height empty in order to use the same width as the input.

4. In **Stream settings** choose **Audio**.

5. In **Audio description name**, change the default name to "AAC audio".

6. In Audio selector name, type the audio selector you created in step 4, that is "My audio source"

   Leave the remaining fields with the default values. Specifically, leave Codec settings as AAC.

Step 7: Save

1. At the bottom of the navigation pane, choose Create channel.

   The channel section reappears and shows the newly created channel, named "MyHLS". The State changes to Creating, then Ready.

2. Stay on this pane for now.

Step 8: Start the Upstream System and the Channel

1. In your upstream system, start streaming the video sources that you set up in step 1. Set them up to push to the two destinations you noted in step 3. For example, rtp://198.51.100.0:5000 and rtp://198.51.100.44:5000.

2. On the channels list, select the channel.

3. Choose Start. The channel State changes to Starting, then to Running.

4. Switch to the web browser tab or window where the AWS Elemental MediaPackage is displayed.

5. Choose the channel link (not the radio button). On the details page, under Endpoints, choose Play. A preview window appears. Start the video. The output from AWS Elemental MediaLive starts playing.

Step 9: Clean up

To avoid extraneous charges, delete this channel and input when you have finished working with it.

1. On the Channels page, select the channel.

2. If needed, choose Stop.

3. Choose Delete.

4. On the Inputs page, select the input.

5. Choose Delete.

Components of AWS Elemental MediaLive

The key building blocks of AWS Elemental MediaLive are *inputs*, *input security groups*, and *channels*. A channel in turn consists of output groups, which contain outputs, which contain video, audio, and captions "encodes".

When a channel is started (run), AWS Elemental MediaLive ingests the input. It then transcodes that video (and the related audio, captions, and metadata) and creates output assets. The information about how to transcode a given input is contained in a channel.

An input security group is a mechanism to prevent unauthorized third parties pushing content into a channel that is associated with "push" input.

Inputs

An *input* is a video asset that is to be transcoded and packaged. It may be associated with an input security group, which provides protection to the input, and with a channel, which provides details about the transcoding and packaging to perform.

AWS Elemental MediaLive supports different types of stream and file inputs (for example, RTP and HLS), The service also provides two ways to ingest the inputs, either through a push model or a pull model. For more information, see [ERROR] BAD/MISSING LINK TEXT.

Channels

In AWS Elemental MediaLive a *channel* is attached to an input (source). A channel contains the details that instruct AWS Elemental MediaLive how to transcode (decode and encode) and package that input into specific outputs. The key components of a channel are an encode, an output, and an output group.

Encodes

An *encode* is the smallest component on the output side of a channel. Each encode contains the instructions for one video asset, one audio asset, or one captions asset that will be created by the transcoding process. Different encodes have different characteristics. For example, one video encode produced from the input may be high resolution while another is low resolution. Or one audio encode may use the AAC audio codec while another uses the Dolby Digital audio codec.

A channel can contain multiple video, audio and captions encodes.

In the following illustration, the red circle represents a video output, the blue circle represents an audio output, and the green circle represents a captions output.

Outputs

An *output* contains the encodes that belong together. For example, one output will contain the combination of video, audio, and captions encodes that make sense for one purpose, while another output will contain a different combination.

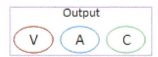

The output holds packaging instructions that apply to all the encodes in that output. For example, the packaging instructions for a UDP output are different from those for an Archive output. The encodes inside the outputs may be the same or different. But the packaging instructions are different.

Output Groups

An *output group* contains related outputs. An output group may contain only one output or it may contain several outputs The output group holds details about the destination for all the outputs in that group.

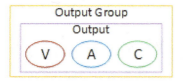

Input Security Groups

An *input security group* is a group you create and associate with specific input types, in order to prevent unauthorized third parties pushing content into a channel. See [ERROR] BAD/MISSING LINK TEXT.

Planning Your Workflow for AWS Elemental MediaLive

To use AWS Elemental MediaLive to transcode a video asset, you follow this basic workflow:

1. You create an input for your video asset.

2. Optionally, you associate the input with an input security group (required only for certain types of inputs).

3. You create a channel in which you identify the input to transcode and specify how AWS Elemental MediaLive should ingest and encode that input.

4. You start (run) your channel, and AWS Elemental MediaLive ingests the input.

5. AWS Elemental MediaLive encodes the input (and any associated audio, captions, and metadata), and then creates the output.

6. You send the output to a packaging and origination service such as AWS Elemental MediaPackage.

- Setting up the Upstream System
- Planning the Input
- Planning the Channel
- Examples of Channel Designs
- Setting up the Downstream System

Setting up the Upstream System

The upstream system is the system that is streaming the video to AWS Elemental MediaLive. A contribution encode "on the ground" is a typical upstream system. You must perform some setup of your upstream system before you start working in AWS Elemental MediaLive.

Here are some guidelines for setting up the upstream video source that is the input into AWS Elemental MediaLive.

- Make sure the upstream system is capable of streaming using one of the supported protocols for input. See [ERROR] BAD/MISSING LINK TEXT. If your chosen protocol is RTP push, make sure to send over RTP, not UDP. The UDP protocol is not supported as an input into AWS Elemental MediaLive.

- Determine if your chosen protocol uses a "push" or a "pull"; see [ERROR] BAD/MISSING LINK TEXT.

- Find out how the input is encoded - the video codecs, audio codecs, and captions formats it uses. Make sure that the input codecs are supported: see [ERROR] BAD/MISSING LINK TEXT. Make sure the captions formats are supported [ERROR] BAD/MISSING LINK TEXT.

- AWS Elemental MediaLive requires redundant sources, so you must provide two video streams. For optimized redundancy, AWS Elemental MediaLive runs each source on different encoders in different Availability Zones (AZs).

  The two streams must be identical in terms of resolution and bit rate. The streams need not be completely synchronized: AWS Elemental MediaLive will accept them if they are not. But AWS Elemental MediaLive will not adjust the streams in order to synchronize them. If an input failure occurs and AWS Elemental MediaLive fails over to the redundant input, then the output maybe skip or repeat.

- For a push input, keep in mind that the input needs to be ready when you start the associated channel. It does not need to be pushing before then.

- For a push input, determine the IP addresses the two streams will be pushing from and make a note of them. You will need this information in order to set up the required input security groups for the AWS Elemental MediaLive inputs that you will create.

- For a pull input, keep in mind that the input needs to be ready to be pulled at the moment that you create the associated channel. It must be ready at this point because AWS Elemental MediaLive verifies that the input can be accessed.

Planning the Input

To plan your input, identify which individual video, audio, and captions assets that you want to extract from the input and which ones you want to omit. For example, you must extract one video file, but you can choose to omit some captions languages.

The rules for extracting input are the following:

- You must extract one and only one video file.

- You can extract zero or more audio files. Typically, you extract multiple audio files so that you can include multiple languages in the output. But you can also extract multiple audio files to extract different audio formats, for example, AAC and Dolby Digital.

- You can extract zero or more captions files. Typically, you extract multiple captions files so that you can include multiple languages in the output. But you can also extract multiple captions to extract different captions formats, for example, DVB-Sub and an external file format such as SRT.

Planning the Channel

1. For the specified input, identify the output protocols (for streaming outputs) or the number of different output file types (for archive outputs).

   For example, you could create a streaming ABR HLS output asset, a streaming non-ABR HLS output asset, and an archive version of the HLS output asset (containing the highest bitrate video). You could also create a streaming ABR Smooth output asset.

2. For the first output asset, identify the number of video encodes that you need.

   - Some output assets consist of one video encode (one set of encoding settings). In this case, you will plan to create an output group that contains one video output.

   - An ABR output asset will have more than one video encode – for example, one high-bitrate video, one medium-bitrate video, and one low-bitrate video. The encoding instructions are identical (for example, they all use H.264) except for the bitrate. In this case, you will plan to create an output group with more than one video output.

3. For the first output asset, identify the audio encodes you need.

   Typically, you need one encode for each language (English, French, etc).

4. For the first output asset, identify the captions your need.

   Typically, you need one encode for each captions language (English, French, etc).

5. Group these encodes into outputs, as described in [ERROR] BAD/MISSING LINK TEXT. Make sure the groupings follow the rules for encodes in outputs.

6. Group the outputs into one output group. For example, group the outputs for the ABR HLS outputs into one output group.

7. Repeat the design of encodes, outputs, and output group for each output asset.

Rules for Encodes in an Output

One output can contain the following:

- A video encode.
- A video encode and one or more audio encodes.
- A video encode and one embedded-type captions.
- A video encode and one or more object-type captions.
- A video encode and one or more audio encodes and one embedded-type captions.
- A video encode and one or more audio encodes and one or more object-type captions.
- An audio encode.
- A sidecar-type captions.

The Result

- Each output in the channel becomes one media asset.

- If a media asset includes manifests, AWS Elemental MediaLive creates one master manifest for each output group and one variant manifest for each output.

Examples of Channel Designs

Following re examples of channel designs. The designs progress from simple designs that where you require only one video offering, to more complex designs for "ABR stacks" where you required several video offerings.

- Non-ABR Asset with Captions Embedded in the Video
- Non-ABR Segmented Asset with Captions as Separate Objects
- Non-ABR Segmented Asset with Captions as Sidecars
- ABR Asset with Captions Embedded in the Video
- ABR Asset with Captions in Sidecars

Non-ABR Asset with Captions Embedded in the Video

For a non-ABR asset, you create the following outputs and encodes in the channel:

One output that contains one video, as many audios as you require, and as many captions assets as you require.

For example:

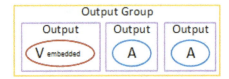

Running this channel produces one segmented media file that will contain the video and audio encodes. In outputs that have manifests, it will also produce one manifest file and one variant manifest file.

Video + Captions + Audio + Audio

Non-ABR Segmented Asset with Captions as Separate Objects

In this example, captions are separate objects, but within the media asset (they are not sidecar files). Captions such as DVB-Sub are set up as separate objects.

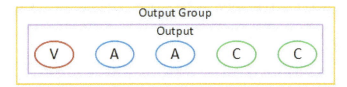

Running this channel produces one segmented media file that contains the video, audio, and captions encodes.

Video + Captions + Captions + Audio + Audio

Non-ABR Segmented Asset with Captions as Sidecars

Regardless of the kind of ABR stack that you create, sidecar captions are always in their own output, one captions (language) per sidecar. But for the audio, the rule is that with an ABR stack, each audio encode is in its own output, while for a non-ABR stack, the audio encodes are in the same output as the video.

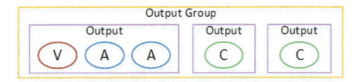

Running this channel produces one media file that contain video and audio, and one media file for each captions asset.

ABR Asset with Captions Embedded in the Video

For an ABR asset, you create the following outputs and encodes:

- Several video outputs, each containing one video encodes (for example, one high-bitrate video, one medium-bitrate video, and one low-bitrate video) and the same embedded captions encode.

- One or more audio encodes (for example, one for each language).

For example:

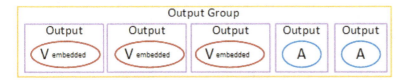

Running this channel will produce five sets of segmented media files, one set for each video output and each audio output. In outputs that have manifests, it will also produce one master manifest and five variant manifests.

ABR Asset with Captions in Sidecars

In this example, the captions (each language) is in its own output:

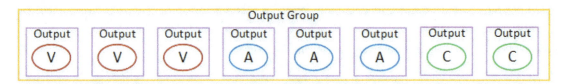

Running this channel will produce seven sets of segmented media files. In outputs that have manifests, it will also produce one manifest file and seven variant manifests.

Setting up the Downstream System

You must set up the device or application that will be downstream of AWS Elemental MediaLive. The downstream system is different for different outputs.

Output Protocol	Typical Downstream Systems
Archive	An AWS S3 bucket.
HLS	A CDN that uses HTTP (or HTTPS) PUT. A CDN that uses HTTP or HTTPS WebDAV. AWS Elemental MediaPackage is an example of this kind of CDN. An Akamai CDN (this always uses HTTP or HTTPS). An AWS Elemental MediaStore container. An AWS S3 bucket. Both AWS Elemental MediaPackage and AWS Elemental MediaStore can serve as CDNs. Or they can serve as origin servers that a CDN such as Amazon CloudFront can pull from.
Microsoft Smooth	A CDN that uses HTTP (or HTTPS) PUT. Typically, the downstream system is a Microsoft IIS server.
UDP	An address that can communicate over UDP or RTP.

The output from AWS Elemental MediaLive will be considered input to this downstream system. You must set up this downstream "input" now because when you are creating the AWS Elemental MediaLive channel you will need the addresses of that input.

AWS Elemental MediaLive always works in redundant mode – it always encodes the input to two destinations (which are inputs from the downstream system's point of view).

1. In your downstream system, set up two inputs.

   - If the downstream system is AWS Elemental MediaPackage, create two AWS Elemental MediaPackage channels. Make a note of the input addresses, the input username, and input password.

   - If the downstream system is an AWS S3 bucket, create two buckets. Make a note of the full path of the buckets.

   - If the downstream system is an AWS Elemental MediaStore container, create two containers. Make a note of the full path of the container and the data plane value of the container.

   - If the downstream system is a CDN, set up so that the CDN expects output at both its inputs. Make a note of the input addresses, and of the input username and input password, if applicable.

2. Put in place some mechanism for ensuring that the output from AWS Elemental MediaLive is arriving successfully:

   - If the output is an archive input, some system downstream of AWS Elemental MediaLive must make sure that one or other of the buckets contains the complete file output.

   - If the output is a stream to AWS S3 or AWS Elemental MediaStore, some system downstream of AWS Elemental MediaLive must make sure that or other of the buckets is continually receiving the streaming output. The system downstream of AWS S3 or AWS Elemental MediaStore should only access complete content.

   - If the downstream system is a CDN, make sure it has logic for detecting a loss in input and switching from one input to the other when that loss is detected.

Working with Input Security Groups

An *input security group* restricts access to an input and prevents unauthorized third parties from pushing content into a channel that is associated with a "push" input. Input security groups are required with RTP and RTMP "push" inputs; they do not apply to "pull" inputs such as HLS. Without the protection of this feature, any third party could push content to an AWS Elemental MediaLive input if they know the IP address and port. Note that setting permissions on the account that owns the channel does not prevent this third-party push; only an input security group prevents it.

An input security group is a set of one or more whitelist rules. Each rule is a range of IP addresses. These IP addresses are allowed to push traffic to the input destinations of a channel (to push traffic to the channel's input).

You create an input security group and attach it to an input.

You can attach an input security group to more than one input. But each input can be associated with only one input security group. In other words, the rule is one input security group to one or more inputs.

Creating an Input Security Group

To create an input security group:

1. Open the AWS Elemental MediaLive console at https://console\.aws\.amazon\.com/medialive?region="region"\.

2. In the navigation pane, choose **Input security groups**.

3. On the **Input security groups** page, choose **Create input security group**.

4. For **New security group**, type one or more IPv4 CIDR blocks. Each CIDR block must include a subnet mask. Separate the entries with commas, or type each entry on a separate line.

   Each item in the list represents one whitelist rule, even if it encompasses several individual addresses. For example, each of the following examples counts as one rule:

   192.0.2.0/24

   192.0.2.111/32

5. Choose **Create**.

Deleting an Input Security Group

Input security groups can be deleted but they cannot be edited.

Important
If you delete an input security group that is associated with an input, the input becomes unusable because the input no longer has the required input security group. Additionally, you can't attach another input security group to the input because you can't edit an input. If the channel that is associated with that input is running, it continues to run and accept input according to the input security group rule that you deleted. But if the channel is stopped (manually or because of a problem), the channel also becomes unusable.

We strongly recommend that you delete an input security group only if it's associated with an input that no longer exists.

To delete an input security group:

1. Open the AWS Elemental MediaLive console at https://console\.aws\.amazon\.com/medialive?region="region"\.

2. In the navigation pane, choose **Input security groups**.

3. On the **Input security groups** page, check the group or groups to delete.

4. Choose **Delete**.

Creating Input

An input is a video asset that is to be transcoded and packaged. The source of the video asset is the "upstream system" – the system in your end-to-end workflow whose activities occur before those of AWS Elemental MediaLive.

AWS Elemental MediaLive supports specific input types. For more information on the types, see [ERROR] BAD/MISSING LINK TEXT.

You must create an AWS Elemental MediaLive input in order to provide information about the source of the video asset.

- Creating an RTP Push Input
- Creating an RTMP Push Input
- Creating an RTMP Pull Input
- Creating an HLS Pull Input

Creating an RTP Push Input

You must create your input before you create the channel that ingests the input.

1. Open the AWS Elemental MediaLive console at https://console\.aws\.amazon\.com/medialive?region="region"\.

2. In the navigation pane, choose **Inputs**.

3. On the **Inputs** page, choose **Create input**.

4. In the **Input details** section, for **Input** name, type a name.

5. For **Input type**, choose **RTP**.

6. In the **Input security group** section, specify a group to associate with this "push" input. You can choose an existing group, or you can create a group. For more information about security groups, see [ERROR] BAD/MISSING LINK TEXT.

7. Choose **Create**.

8. AWS Elemental MediaLive adds the input to the list of inputs and automatically creates two destinations (one primary and one redundant). These destinations include the port 5000. For example, rtp://198.51.100.0:5000 and rtp://198.51.100.44:5000. These are the two locations where the upstream system must push the source.

   Provide the upstream system with these locations.

Creating an RTMP Push Input

1. Open the AWS Elemental MediaLive console at https://console\.aws\.amazon\.com/medialive?region="region"\.

2. In the navigation pane, choose **Inputs**.

3. On the **Inputs** page, choose **Create input**.

4. In the **Input details** section, for **Input** name, type a name.

5. For **Input type**, choose **RTMP (push)**.

6. In the **Input security group** section, specify a group to associate with this push input. You can choose an existing group, or you can create a group. For more information about security groups, see [ERROR] BAD/MISSING LINK TEXT.

7. In the **Input destinations** section, type the final portion of the two destination locations (one primary and one redundant) on AWS Elemental MediaLive. For example, `movies/classic`. Don't include a leading slash. For example, don't type `/movies/classic`.

    Typically, you enter the same value in both destinations; the difference in the two destinations will exist in the network portion that will be auto-generated.

8. Choose **Create**.

9. AWS Elemental MediaLive adds the input to the list of inputs and automatically creates two destinations ; the destinations include the final portion you specified. These destinations include the port 1935. For example, rtmp://198.51.100.0:1935/movies/classic and rtmp://198.51.100.66:1935/movies/classic. These are the two locations where the upstream system must push the source.

    Provide the upstream system with these locations.

Creating an RTMP Pull Input

1. Open the AWS Elemental MediaLive console at https://console\.aws\.amazon\.com/medialive?region="region"\.

2. In the navigation pane, choose **Inputs**.

3. On the **Inputs** page, choose **Create input**.

4. In the **Input details** section, for **Input** name, type a name.

5. For **Input type**, choose **RTMP (pull)**.

6. In the **Input sources** section, type the full URI of the two locations where AWS Elemental MediaLive will pull the source from. Obtain these locations from the upstream system. For example, `rtmp://203.0.113.0:1935/movies/classic` and `rtmp://203.0.113.254:1935/movies/classic`.

   Also, enter the user name and Amazon EC2 password key for accessing the RTMP location. These credentials are stored on the Amazon EC2 Systems Manager Parameter Store. For more information, see [ERROR] BAD/MISSING LINK TEXT.

7. Choose **Create**.

8. AWS Elemental MediaLive adds the input to the list of inputs. The sources don't appear in the list, but if you choose the **Name** link, the details page shows these sources.

Creating an HLS Pull Input

1. Open the AWS Elemental MediaLive console at https://console\.aws\.amazon\.com/medialive?region="region"\.

2. In the navigation pane, choose **Inputs**.

3. On the **Inputs** page, choose **Create input**.

4. In the **Input details** section, for **Input** name, type a name.

5. For **Input type**, choose **HLS**.

6. In the **Input sources **section, type the full URI of the two locations where AWS Elemental MediaLive will pull the M3U8 manifest source from. Obtain these locations from the upstream system. Enter the location of the M3U8 manifest in one of these formats:

   - For a location that supports HTTP or HTTPS, type an HTTP or HTTPS URI. For example, `https://203.0.113.0/newschannel/anytownusa.m3u8` and `https://203.0.113.254/newschannel/anytownusa.m3u8`.

   - For a manifest that is stored on AWS Elemental MediaStore, the URI must include the data endpoint for the container. For example, the M3U8 file is called mlaw.m3u8 and it is stored on the container "movies" in the folder path "premium/canada". The URL for the container might be **eri39n.data.mediastore.us-west-2.amazonaws.com**. The value you enter in this field would be **mediastoressl://eri39n.data.mediastore.us-west-2.amazonaws.com/premium/canada/mlaw.m3u8**.

   - For a manifest that is stored on Amazon S3, type the protocol as **s3** or **s3ssl**, and then type the bucket and object for the manifest. For example, `s3:/movies/mlaw.m3u8` and `s3:/movies/redundant/mlaw.m3u8`.

7. If you are using a secure connection (S3SSL), you must also enter the user name and EC2 password key for accessing the location. These credentials are stored on the Amazon EC2 Systems Manager Parameter Store. For more information, see [ERROR] BAD/MISSING LINK TEXT.

8. Choose **Create**.

9. AWS Elemental MediaLive adds the input to the list of inputs. The sources don't appear in the list, but if you choose the **Name** link, the details page shows these sources.

Creating a Channel from Scratch

A channel contains the details that instruct AWS Elemental MediaLive how to transcode (decode and encode) and package your input into specific outputs.

To create a channel you must provide details about inputs, about one or more output groups and their destinations, about the outputs in each output group, and about the video, audio and caption encodes in each output.

There are three ways to create a channel:

- **From scratch.** See below
- **Using a built-in or custom template.** See [ERROR] BAD/MISSING LINK TEXT.
- **By cloning an existing channel.** See [ERROR] BAD/MISSING LINK TEXT.
- Step 1: Get Started
- Step 2: Set Up the Input
- Step 3: Set Global Settings and Optional Features
- Step 4: Create Output Groups
- Step 5: Create Outputs
- Step 6: Set up the Video Encode
- Step 7: Set up the Audio Encodes
- Step 8: Set up the Captions Encodes
- Step 9: Save

Step 1: Get Started

The first step to creating a channel is to select the role that AWS Elemental MediaLive will use with this channel.

1. Before creating a channel, make sure you have created the input [ERROR] BAD/MISSING LINK TEXT that you will attach to the channel.

2. On the console, choose **Channels **in the navigation pane.

3. In the content pane, choose **Create Channel**. The **Create channel** page appears.

4. Complete the fields in the **Channel and input details **pane, see below for details on specific fields.

5. When ready, go to the next step.

IAM Role and Remember ARN

You must choose a role for AWS Elemental MediaLive to assume, when it is working with this channel. If you do not choose a role, you will not be able to create the channel. Here are some tips for choosing the role:

- If your organization has an administrator whose job is to manage this service, that administrator has likely set up one or more roles. Ask the administrator or your manager which role to use. Or if only one rule is listed in **Use existing role**, choose that role.

- If your organization does not have a service administrator, you may have to create a role yourself and then choose it. You can create and choose the default role, called MediaLiveAccessRole. To first check if someone else has already created this role (only one person needs to create it for all users in your AWS account), look at **Create role from template**.

  - If this option is grayed out, this task has been done. In this case, choose **Use existing role **and then select MediaLiveAccessRole from the list.

  - If this option is not grayed out, choose **Create role from template** and choose **Create IAM role**. Then choose that role from the list. If AWS Elemental MediaLive does not let you create the role, speak to an AWS IAM administrator about your permissions.

- Check **Remember ARN** if you want the selected ARN to appear first in the list the next time you create a channel.

For details about ARNs and the MediaLiveAccessRole role, see [ERROR] BAD/MISSING LINK TEXT.

Step 2: Set Up the Input

In this step, you select the input to attach to the channel and provide information about how to ingest the input.

1. On the **Create channel **navigation pane, choose **Channel and input details**.

2. In the **Input specification** section, change the fields to match your input. See below for details on the fields in this section.

3. In the **Channel input** section, select an existing input. More fields appear. Complete the fields that apply to the selected input. See below for details on specific fields.

4. In the **Input settings** section, complete the fields as required. For details on a field, choose the Info link next to the field.

   - For most fields, the default values will work.

   - However, if you want to include audio and captions in the outputs, you must complete the **Audio selectors **and **Caption selectors** sections; the defaults do not specify enough information.

5. When ready, go to the next step.

Input Specification Settings

This section includes three fields that characterize the video in the input you intend to use with this channel. The values in these fields are used to calculate the charges you will incur on the input side and to ensure that AWS Elemental MediaLive allocates sufficient processing resources, when you run this channel.

All the fields provide options that cover ranges, with the lowest range shown first and the highest shown last. Lower ranges imply lower processing requirements, higher ranges imply higher requirements.

For each field, make sure that you choose an option that meets or exceeds the requirements of your input. If you do not, then AWS Elemental MediaLive may not allocate sufficient processing resources. If you are not sure about the processing requirements of your input, choose a higher option. For example, if you are not sure of the bitrate and you are trying to choose between 10 MBPS and 20 MBPS, then choose 20 MBPS, to be on the safe side. Even with codecs, this advice applies: if you are not sure if your input is AVC (H.264) or HEVC (H.265), then choose HEVC.

AWS Elemental MediaLive uses these values for billing and resource allocation purposes: you will pay for the option you specify. For example, if you specify HD but the input is actually SD, you will be charged for HD.

But AWS Elemental MediaLive does not use these values for determining what is actually in the video for decoding purposes. At ingest time, it still inspects the video to detect the source codec, resolution, and bitrate.

Channel input - RTP Push Input

- Look at the **Input destinations** section. It shows the two locations on AWS Elemental MediaLive that the upstream system will push the source to, when the channel is running. These locations were automatically generated when you created the input.

  For example, **rtp://198.51.100.0:5000** and **rtp://198.51.100.44:5000**.

- Choose **Input security group**; more information appears. Make sure that an input security group is listed.

  If a group is specified, you can continue.

  If no group is specified, you cannot use this input because it has no input security group attached. Typically, this situation occurs if, for example, you have input A attached to input security group B and then you delete B. Input A is no longer useable. You must recreate the input and attach an input security group to it before you can associate it with a channel you are creating.

Channel input - RTMP Push Input

- Look at the **Input destinations** section. It shows the two locations on AWS Elemental MediaLive that the upstream system will push the source to, when the channel is running. These locations were automatically generated when you created the input. Each location consists of an address portion that was automatically generated, appended by a folder you specified when you created the input.

  For example, **rtmp://198.51.100.0:1935/movies/classic** and **rtmp://198.51.100.45:1935/movies/-classic**.

- Choose **Input security group**; more information appears. Make sure that an input security group is listed.

  If a group is specified, you can continue.

  If no group is specified, you cannot use this input because it has no input security group attached. Typically, this situation occurs if, for example, you have input A attached to input security group B and then you delete B. Input A is no longer useable. You must recreate the input and attach an input security group to it before you can associate it with a channel you are creating.

Channel input - RTMP Pull Input

Look at the **Input destinations** section. It shows the locations of the source video; you specified these locations when you created the input.

For example, **rtmp://203.0.113.0:1935/movies/classic** and **rtmp://203.0.113.254:1935/movies/classic**.

**Channel input - HLS Pull Input **

Look at the **Input sources** section. It shows the locations of the source video; you specified these locations when you created the input.

For example, **https://203/.0/.113/.0/newchannel/anytownusa/.m3u8** and **https://203/.0/.113/.254/newchannel/anytownusa/.m3u8** (for an HTTPS pull).

Or **mediastoressl://eri39n.data.mediastore.us-west-2.amazonaws.com/premium/canada/m-law.m3u8** and **mediastoressl://eri39n.data.mediastore.us-west-2.amazonaws.com/redundant/premium/canada/mlaw.m3u8** (for an AWS Elemental MediaStore pull).

Input Settings - Network Input Settings

Complete this section only if the input is HLS.

Input Settings - Other Settings

The fields that are not within the **Network input settings** section apply to all inputs.

Input Settings - Video selector

This section lets you identify the video to extract from the input, and lets you enable the optional color space feature.

- In Video selector, choose Video selector. More fields appear.

- **Selector settings**: This field lets you identify the video to ingest.

  With RTP input, this field is optional but strongly recommended because the input may contain more than one video. If you do not identify the video, AWS Elemental MediaLive selects the first video it finds, which may result in undesired content, especially in a live streaming context. If you want to explicitly identify the video but do not know its program ID or PID, speak to the content provider.

  With all other input types, this field is optional because the input only ever contains one video.

  You can specify the video by specifying a program ID (which typically exist in an MPTS input) or by specifying a PID (which exist in both MPTS and SPTS inputs).

Keep in mind that there is no button to add more video selectors because you can only extract one video asset from the input.

- **Color space** and **Color space usage**: These fields let you configure the optional color space feature.

Input Settings - Audio selectors

This section is required if you want to extract audio from the input. You create one or more audio selectors to identify the audio to extract. Typically, you identify different languages from the input, but you could also extract different audio codecs (such as AAC and Dolby).

For each audio you want to extract, choose **Add audio selector**. Complete the fields that appear to identify the location of the audio and to specify optional handling of the audio.

Input Settings - Caption selectors

This section is required if you want to extract captions from the input or to specify an external file as the source of the captions. You create one or more captions selectors to identify the captions to extract. Typically, you identify different languages in each selector, but you could also identify different captions formats.

For each caption item you want to extract or include, choose **Add captions **selector. For detailed information on setting up input for captions, see [ERROR] BAD/MISSING LINK TEXT, specifically [ERROR] BAD/MISSING LINK TEXT.

Step 3: Set Global Settings and Optional Features

AWS Elemental MediaLive has several *settings* that apply globally to all outputs; these settings are therefore located in this section, rather than in individual output groups and outputs.

AWS Elemental MediaLive also has *features* that are optional but that apply globally if they are enabled.

1. On the Create channel navigation pane, choose General Settings.

2. Set these optional features and global settings as needed. See below for details on the groups of settings.

3. When done with these fields, go to the next step.

Avail Blanking

Optional feature. You can set up to blank out the output video during ad avails. For details, see [ERROR] BAD/MISSING LINK TEXT.

Avail Configuration

Optional feature. You can modify the way that AWS Elemental MediaLive handles SCTE-35ad avail messages, or you can leave the default behavior. See [ERROR] BAD/MISSING LINK TEXT for information on the default behavior and modifying that behavior.

Blackout Slate

Optional feature. You can set up to black out the output video as specified by program metadata, if that metadata is present in the input. For details, see [ERROR] BAD/MISSING LINK TEXT .

Global Configuration

Global configuration settings. In this section, complete the first three fields as appropriate. For details on each field, choose the Info link next to the field.

Global Configuration - Input Loss Behavior

Global configuration settings. The Input Loss Behavior fields change how AWS Elemental MediaLive handles input loss. When AWS Elemental MediaLive detects that the input has not arrived within the expected time, it repeats the previous frame for a configurable number of milliseconds (from zero to forever). When that time expires, it displays a black frame for a configurable number of milliseconds (from zero to forever). When that time expires, it switches to a specified slate or to a specified color. When input resumes, the normal ingest continues.

You can change this behavior: in Input Loss Behavior, choose Input Loss Behavior. The default values are shown in the fields that appear. Change the fields as desired. If you want to later switch back to the default behavior, simply set Input Loss Behavior to Disabled.

Image Inserter

Optional feature. You can insert static graphic overlays on the output video.

Timecode Config

Global configuration settings. This section lets you specify the timecode for the output. This timecode does not have to be the same as the timecode you specified for the input . The input timecode fields are used to notify AWS Elemental MediaLive what timecode is present in the input, so that AWS Elemental MediaLive can find it, and read it or apply it correctly. The output timecode fields are used to specify the timecode format AWS Elemental MediaLive must apply to the output.

Step 4: Create Output Groups

Create the output groups you identified when you planned the channel. AWS Elemental MediaLive supports different output types; see [ERROR] BAD/MISSING LINK TEXT.

Creating an Archive Output Group

Follow these steps if, when you were planning the channel, you determined that you want to include an archive output group.

1. On the **Create channel **navigation pane, go to the **Output groups** section and choose **Add**. The content pane changes to show the **Add output group **section.

2. Choose **Archive** and choose **Confirm**. More sections appear.

3. Complete the fields as described in [ERROR] BAD/MISSING LINK TEXT.

4. When you have entered all the information for one output group, create another output group, if desired. Otherwise, go to the next step.

Fields for Archive Group

Archive Settings

- Enter a name for the output group. For example, **Sports Game 10122017 ABR** or **tvchannel59**.
- In **Archive settings**, choose **Additional settings** and complete the **Rollover Interval** field , if desired. This field interacts with the fields in the **Archive destinations** section lower down on this panel.

Archive Destinations

You must specify the destinations for this output. Each destination is a bucket and object in an AWS S3 account. You must be set up so that AWS Elemental MediaLive can access your AWS S3 account; see [ERROR] BAD/MISSING LINK TEXT.

You must specify two destinations because AWS Elemental MediaLive works in redundant mode for outputs: it requires two destinations. The URL is one piece of the information use for the location and filenames of the output file; see [ERROR] BAD/MISSING LINK TEXT .

Archive Outputs

This section contains fields related to the encoding of the video, audio, and captions in the output, and related to the packaging and delivery of the output.

- Choose **Add output** if you want more than one output in this output group. An **Output** line is added for each output. Setup of the individual outputs is described in [ERROR] BAD/MISSING LINK TEXT.
- In the **Name modifier** field for each output, type a modifier, if appropriate. See [ERROR] BAD/MISSING LINK TEXT for uses for this field.

About Archive Locations and Filenames

The location of archive output files is controlled by several fields in the Archive output group and the individual outputs.

- The two **URL** fields in the **Archive destinations** section. The URL consists of a *protocol* portion, a *path *portion and a *base filename *portion.

  For example, assume the URL is `s3ssl://interviews/3series/Delivery/3633_WangXiuLan`.

  s3ssl:// is the protocol. The protocol is always **s3ssl://**, to indicate that the destination is an AWS S3 bucket.

  `interviews/3series/Delivery/` is the path. The path is required and consists a bucket and folders, terminated by a slash.

  `3633_WangXiuLan` is the base filename. The base filename is optional. If you omit it, AWS Elemental MediaLive uses the name of the input as the base filename.

- The **Name modifier **field in the **Archive outputs **section. Required. The string forms part of the filename.
- The **Extension** field in the **Archive outputs **section. The extension for the filename. Required only if you do not want to use the default (`.ts`).

- The **Rollover interval **field in the **Archive settings **section. Required. For example, **600** divides the output into separate files, each 600 seconds (10 minutes) long. Each filename includes a 6-digit sequential counter, 000000, 000001, and so on.

The values from these fields are put together to form the location:

protocol path base_filename name_modifier sequential_counter extension

For more information, see the examples.

Archive Examples

These examples show how to set up the fields relating to locations. They do not show how to set up other fields such as field in the individual outputs.

Example 1

You want to create an archive of the streaming output from TV channel 59. You want to store the output in the S3 bucket named "channel59" and want to break up the stream into 10 minute chunks.

Field	Value
Rollover interval field in Archive settings section	600
Primary URL in Archive destinations section	s3ssl://channel59/delivery/program
Backup URL in Archive destinations section	s3ssl://channel59/backup/programUsing "delivery" and "backup" as folder names is only an example.
Name modifier in Archive outputs section	_dtFor information on identifiers for variable data (such as dt), see [ERROR] BAD/MISSING LINK TEXT
Extension in Archive outputs section	Leave blank in order to use the default (.ts).

Result: the output will be broken into files of 10 minutes (600 seconds) each. Each file will have a filename of `program` plus the time that the channel started plus a counter (000000, 000001, and so on), plus the filename extension. For example:

The first file will be `program_20171012T033162.000000.ts`

The second file will be `program_20171012T033162.000001.ts`

and so on.

Each file will be stored in both `s3ssl://channel59/delivery` and `s3ssl://channel59/backup`.

Example 2

You want to create an archive of highlights from the curling game that are also being streamed (in a separate HLS output group). You want to create three outputs: one that has audio languages for Europe, one for audio languages for Asia, and one for audio languages for Africa. You want to store the outputs in the AWS S3 bucket named "sports/highlights/curling". You want to break up the stream into 5 minute chunks.

Field	Value
Rollover interval field in Archive settings section	300
Primary URL in Archive destinations section	s3ssl://sports/delivery/highlights/curling/10312017In this example, the **10312017** folder is set to match today's date.
Backup URL in Archive destinations section	s3ssl://sports/backup/highlights/curling/10312017Using "delivery" and "backup" as folder names is only an example.

Field	Value
Name modifier in Archive outputs section	Choose **Add output** twice: two more Output lines are added to this section, for a total of three lines. In each line, enter a modifier: **_audiogroup1**, **_audiogroup2**, and **_audiogroup3**.
Extension in Archive outputs section	Leave blank in order to use the default (.ts).

Result: three separate sets of files will be created for each output. Each file will have a filename of 10312017 plus the modifier, plus the sequence counter, plus the filename extension. For example:

`10312017_audiogroup1.000000.ts,` `10312017_audiogroup2.000000.ts` and `10312017_audiogroup3.000000.ts.`

`10312017_audiogroup1.000001.ts,` `10312017_audiogroup2.000001.ts` and `10312017_audiogroup3.000001.ts.`

and so on.

The files will be stored in both `s3ssl://sports/delivery/highlights/curling` and `s3ssl://sports/backup/highlights/curling`.

Creating an HLS Output Group

Follow these steps if, when you were planning the channel, you determined that you want to include an HLS output group.

1. On the **Create channel** navigation pane, go to the** Output groups** section and choose **Add**. The content pane changes to show the **Add output** group section.

2. Choose **HLS** and choose **Confirm**. More sections appear.

3. Complete the fields as described in [ERROR] BAD/MISSING LINK TEXT.

4. When you have entered all the information for one output group, create another output group, if desired. Otherwise, go to the next step.

HLS Settings

- Enter a name for the output group. For example, **Sports Game 10122017 ABR** or **tvchannel59**.

- In **CDN settings**, set the value to specify the type of connection that is being used to write to the destination URLs (specified in the HLS destinations section lower down on this panel). The options are:

  - **Hls basic put**: To send to a CDN that uses HTTP (or HTTPS) PUT. Or to send to an AWS S3 bucket (`s3://` or `s3ssl://`)

  - **Hls media store**: An AWS Elemental MediaStore container (`mediastoressl://`).

  - **Hls akamai**: An Akamai CDN (this always uses HTTP or HTTPS).

  - **Hls webdav**: A CDN that uses HTTP or HTTPS WebDAV. AWS Elemental MediaPackage can be the destination for HLS output; it uses WebDAV.

  When you have selected the CDN type, more fields appear, appropriate to the type of connection. For details on a field, choose the Info link next to the field.

  The CDN is one piece of the information used for the location and filenames of the manifest and media files.

- Change the value of **Input loss action**, if desired.

- Complete the **Caption language mappings **fields only if the output includes embedded captions.

- Complete the **Location** section to specify the location and organization of the manifest and asset files at the publishing point. The fields in this section work with the fields in the HLS destinations.

- Complete the **Manifest and segments **section to change the default setup of the HLS manifest and the segmentation of outputs.

- Complete the **DRM** section only if you are setting up for DRM using a static key to encrypt the output. In **Key provider **settings, choose **Static key** and complete all the other fields as appropriate. For details on a field, choose the Info link next to the field.

  In a static key setup, you enter an encryption key in this section (along with other configuration data) and then give that key to the other party (for example, by sending it in an email). Static key is not really a DRM solution and is not particularly secure.

  AWS Elemental MediaLive supports only static key as an encryption option. To use a DRM solution with a key provider, you must deliver the output to AWS Elemental MediaPackage (in other words, set up AWS Elemental MediaPackage as the destination for the output) and then encrypt the video using AWS Elemental MediaPackage . See the documentation for AWS Elemental MediaPackage.

- Complete the **Ad marker** section if you are including SCTE-35 ad messages in the output. See [ERROR] BAD/MISSING LINK TEXT and specifically [ERROR] BAD/MISSING LINK TEXT.

- Complete the **Captions** section.

- Complete the **ID3** section if applicable.

Fields for HLS Group

HLS Destinations

You must specify the destination URLs for this output. You must specify two destination URLs because AWS Elemental MediaLive works in redundant mode for outputs: it requires two destinations.

The URL is one piece of the information used for the location and filenames of the manifest and media files.

HLS Outputs

This section contains fields related to the encoding of the video, audio, and captions in the output, and related to the packaging and delivery of the output.

- Choose **Add output** if you want more than one output in this output group. An **Output** line is added for each output. Setup of the individual outputs is described in [ERROR] BAD/MISSING LINK TEXT.

- In the **Name modifier** field for each output, enter a modifier, if appropriate. See [ERROR] BAD/MISSING LINK TEXT for uses for this field.

About HLS Destinations and Filenames

HLS output consists of a manifest, one rendition manifest for each output in the output group, and media files: one set of .ts files for each output, and optionally one or more captions files for each output.

For example, one manifest file called `curling.m3u8`, one rendition manifest called `curling_high.m3u8`, and many `.ts` files containing the video and audio (each file containing one segment of a specified number of seconds) and three `.vtt` files for English, French, and Spanish Web-VTT captions.

The location of these files is controlled by several fields in the HLS output group and the individual outputs:

- The fields in the **CDN** section.

  The main field specifies the type of connection to the CDN, which is the downstream system that is the destination for the HLS output. For example, the CDN is of type HLS WebDAV if the destination is AWS Elemental MediaPackage. The other fields in this section provide connection details.

- The two **URL** fields in the **HLS destinations** section.

  The URL consists of a *protocol* portion, a *path *portion and a *base filename *portion.

  For example, assume the URL is `https://sports/curling`.

  `https://` is the protocol portion. The protocol is required and must be correct for the CDN you specified. For example, **https://** is correct if the CDN type is **Hls basic put** or **Hls akamai** or **Hls webdav**.

  - `http://` or `https://` if you selected **Hls basic put** as the CDN and you are sending to send to a CDN that uses HTTP (or HTTPS) PUT.

  - `s3://` or `s3ssl://` if you selected **Hls basic put** as the CDN and you are sending to send to an AWS S3 bucket.

  - `mediastoressl://` if you selected **Hls media store** as the CDN.

  - `http://` or `https://` if you selected **Hls akamai** as the CDN.

  - `http://` or `https://` if you selected **Hls webdav** as the CDN and you are sending to a server using WebDAV or you are sending to AWS Elemental MediaPackage.

`sports/` is the path portion. The path is required and consists of the folders, terminated by a slash. It identifies the location of the manifest and media files.

`curling` is the base filename. It is used in the manifest filenames and media filenames. The base filename is optional. If you omit it, AWS Elemental MediaLive uses the name of the input as the base filename.

- The **Name modifier **field in the **HLS outputs **section.

Required only in output groups with more than one output. For example, **_high**. Used in the rendition manifest filenames and in media filenames.

For example, following from the example above, the manifest file would be `curling`, rendition manifest files would be `curling_high` and `curling_low`. Media video files would by `curling_high.00001.ts`, `curling_high.00002.ts`, and so on for output 1, and `curling_medium.00001.ts`, `curling_medium .00002.ts`, and so on for output 2.

- The **Segment modifier** field in the **Output settings** section of each individual output.

Always optional. For example, **_high**. Used only in the media filenames. Typically used instead of **Name modifier**, when you have only one output in the output group and you want a modifier in the media but not in the manifest.

For example, following from the example above, the manifest file would be `curling`, the rendition manifest file would be `curling`, and media video files would by `curling_high.00001.ts`, `curling_high.00002.ts`.

- The **Base URL manifest** field and **Base URL** field in the **Location **section.

Always optional. These fields are typically used only for non-standard manifests.

- The **Directory structure** field in the **Location** section.

Optional. Used only to create subdirectories for the media files. Creates one subdirectory for each output, then creates sub-subdirectories according to the Segments per subdirectory field.

For example, the high-resolution media files would go in subdirectories with the same name as each rendition manifest: `curling_high` and `curling_low`. Inside each subdirectory would be a sub-subdirectory named 00001 (for the first set of media files), 00002 (for the next set of media files), and so on.

HLS Example

This example shows how to set up the fields relating to destinations. They do not show how to set up other fields such as field in the individual outputs.

You want to stream the curling game to . You want toAWS Elemental MediaPackage create three outputs: high, medium, and low bitrate.

Field	Value
CDN settings in HLS settings section	hls webdavThis is the type of connection that AWS Elemental MediaPackage uses. Change the other CDN fields that appear, or leave the defaults.
Location in HLS settings section	Leave the defaults in all the fields; these fields are not used in this example.
Primary URL in HLS destinations section	For example, https://62e3c93793c034c/.mediapackage/.us/-west/-2/.amazonaws/.com/in/v1/9378dje8/channel The URLs are the Input URLS from the channel in AWS Elemental MediaPackage. As discussed in [ERROR] BAD/MISSING LINK TEXT, the input in AWS Elemental MediaPackage is identical to the output from AWS Elemental MediaLive. This input URL must already exist in AWS Elemental MediaPackage.Note that in AWS Elemental MediaPackage, URLs always end in "channel", so the base filename in AWS Elemental MediaLive must be "channel".
Credentials in Primary URL in HLS destinations section	The protocol for AWS Elemental MediaPackage is HTTPS, which is a secure connection, so you must type a username and a password that is known to AWS Elemental MediaPackage. For the password, enter the EC2 Parameter store name value (not the actual password). For more information, see Access to Amazon EC2 Systems Manager Parameter Store.
Backup URL in HLS destinations section	For example, https://60dei849783734c/.mediapackage/.us/-west/-2/.amazonaws/.com/in/v1/6da5ba717b357a/channel
Credentials in Backup URL in HLS destinations section	Type a username and password, as for the primary URL. The credentials are probably the same as for the primary URL, but they may not be.
Name modifier in HLS outputs section	Choose **Add output** twice: two more Output lines are added to this section, for a total of three lines. In each line, enter a modifier: **_high**, **_medium**, and **_low**.

Result: Files will be created with the following names:

- One master manifest: `channel.m3u8`

- One rendition manifest for each output: `channel_high.m3u8`, `channel_medium.m3u8`, `channel_low.m3u8`
- TS files for each output:
  - `channel_high.00001.ts`, `channel_high.00002.ts`, `channel_high.00003.ts`, and so on.
  - `channel_medium.00001.ts`, `channel_medium.00002.ts`, `channel_medium.00003.ts`, and so on.
  - `channel_low.00001.ts`, `channel_low.00002.ts`,`channel_low.00003.ts`, and so on.

The files will be published to both URL inputs on AWS Elemental MediaPackage .

Creating a Microsoft Smooth Output Group

Follow these steps if, when you were planning the channel, you determined that you want to include a Microsoft Smooth output group.

1. On the **Create channel **navigation pane, go to the **Output groups** section and choose **Add**. The content pane changes to show the **Add output group** section.

2. Choose **Microsoft Smooth **and choose **Confirm**. More sections appear.

3. Complete the fields as described in [ERROR] BAD/MISSING LINK TEXT.

4. When you have entered all the information for one output group, create another output group, if desired. Otherwise, go to the next step.

Fields for Microsoft Smooth Group

Microsoft Smooth Settings

- Enter a name for the output group. For example, **Sports Game 10122017 ABR** or **tvchannel59**.

- Choose **General configuration** if you want to change the default setup of the Microsoft Smooth manifest and fragments. For details on a field, choose the Info link next to the field.

- Choose **Event configuration** if you want to change the configuration of the event information that is sent to the Microsoft IIS server. For details on a field, choose the Info link next to the field.

- Choose **Timecode configuration** if you want to change the default setup of the timecode and timestamp that will be used in all the outputs in this output group. For details on a field, choose the Info link next to the field.

- Choose **Sparse track** if you want all the outputs in this output group to include the SCTE-35 messages that are already present in the input. The messages will be included in a sparse track. For details on a field, choose the Info link next to the field. For details, see [ERROR] BAD/MISSING LINK TEXT.

Microsoft Smooth Destinations

Specify the URLs for two destinations. You must specify two destinations because AWS Elemental MediaLive works in redundant mode for outputs: it requires two destinations. The URLs must use the HTTP or HTTPS protocol. Do not include the port.

Specify the path portion of the destination as /folders/basefilename. The basefilename will be used as the first part of the filename of all the files for all outputs in this output group. Or specify it as /folders/. In this case, the name of the input will be used for the filenames.

Microsoft Smooth Outputs

This section contains fields related to the encoding of the video, audio, and captions in the output, and related to the packaging and delivery of the output.

- Choose **Add output** if you want more than one output in this output group. An **Output** line is added for each output. Setup of the individual outputs is described in [ERROR] BAD/MISSING LINK TEXT.

- In the **Name modifier** field for each output, enter a modifier, if appropriate. See examples for uses for this field.

Microsoft Smooth Example

These examples show how to set up the fields relating to destination. They do not show how to set up other fields such as field in the individual outputs.

You want to stream the curling game to an origin server that supports Microsoft Smooth. You want to create three outputs: high, medium, and low bitrate.

Field	Value
Primary URL in Microsoft Smooth destinations section	For example, https://192/.0/.2/.0/sports/curling/dFor information on identifiers for variable data (such as d), see [ERROR] BAD/MISSING LINK TEXT.
Credentials in Primary URL in HLS destinations section	The protocol is HTTPS, which is a secure connection, so you must type a username and a password that is known to the origin server. For the password, enter the EC2 Parameter store name value (not the actual password). For more information, see Access to Amazon EC2 Systems Manager Parameter Store.
Backup URL in Microsoft Smooth destinations section	For example, https://192/.0/.2/.230/sports/curling/d
Credentials in Backup URL in HLS destinations section	Type a username and password, as for the primary URL. The credentials are probably the same as for the primary URL, but they may not be.
Name modifier in Microsoft Smooth outputs section	Leave blank; in this example, a name modifier is not used.

Result: Assuming the channel is run on November 30, 2017, then files will be created with the following names:

- One master manifest:20171130.isml

- A set of video, audio and captions for output 1: 20171130_high.ismv, 20171130_high.isma, 20171130_high.ismt

- A set of video, audio and captions for output 2: 20171130_medium.ismv, 20171130_medium.isma, 20171130_medium.ismt

- A set of video, audio and captions for output 3: 20171130_low.ismv, 20171130_low.isma, 20171130_low.ismt

The files will be published to both destinations: https://192.0.2.0/sports/curling/d and https://192.0.2.230/sports/curling/d.

Creating a UDP Output Group

Follow these steps if, when you were planning the channel, you determined that you want to include a UDP output group.

1. On the **Create channel** navigation pane, go to the **Output groups** section and choose **Add**. The content pane changes to show the **Add output group** section.

2. Choose **UDP** and choose **Confirm**. More sections appear.

3. Complete the fields as described below.

4. When you have entered all the information for one output group, create another output group, if desired. Otherwise, go to the next step.

UDP settings

- Enter a name for the output group. For example, **Sports Game 10122017 ABR** or **tvchannel59**.
- Change the value of **Input loss action**, if desired.
- Complete the **ID3** fields if applicable.

UDP destinations

Specify the URLs for two destinations. You must specify two destinations because AWS Elemental MediaLive works in redundant mode for outputs: it requires two destinations. The URLs must use the RTP or UDP protocol and must include a port number.

If FEC is enabled (this field is in the Output panel, not the Output group panel), then leave space between the port numbers for the two destinations. For example, if one destination is **rtp://192.0.2.0:5000**, then assume that FEC will also use port 5002 and 5004. So the lowest possible port number for the other destination is 5005: **rtp://192.0.2.230:5005**.

UDP outputs

This section contains fields related to the encoding of the video, audio, and captions in the output, and related to the packaging and delivery of the output.

Choose **Add output** if you want more than one output in this output group. An **Output** line is added for each output. Setup of the individual outputs is described in [ERROR] BAD/MISSING LINK TEXT.

Step 5: Create Outputs

Every output group contains one or more outputs. Each output contains the individual video, audio, and captions encodes as well as configuration information for the type of output. For example, it contains configuration information specific to an HLS output.

This section describes how to create and configure the outputs and assumes you have created the output group.

1. On the **Output group** panel, the **Output** section is set up by default with one output. If you need to create more outputs (as determined when you planned the channel, then choose **Add Output** as many times as required. A new output line is added.

2. Choose the **Settings** link beside the first output line. The content panel shows the fields for that output.

   The panel for all output types shows two sections: **Output settings** and **Stream settings**. The fields in **Output settings** are different for each output type. The fields in **Stream settings** are the same for all output types.

3. Complete both sections as described below.

4. When done, go to the next output in this output group. When you have set up all the outputs in the output group, go to the outputs in the next output group.

When you have set up all outputs, go to the next step.

- Settings for an Archive Output
- Settings for an HLS Output
- Settings for a Microsoft Smooth Output
- Settings for a UDP Output

Settings for an Archive Output

Output Settings Section

1. Complete the Name modifier field as described in [ERROR] BAD/MISSING LINK TEXT.

2. Leave Extension blank; it will always be set to m2ts.

3. In the fields under Container Settings, change any values as desired. For details on a field, choose the Info link next to the field.

4. In the fields under PID settings, change any values as desired. For details on a field, choose the Info link next to the field.

Streams Section

In Stream settings, decide if you need to create more encodes for this output, based on the workflow you planned. By default, each output is set up with one video encode and one audio encode. Select the appropriate Add button or Delete button to set up the output with the encodes – video, audio, captions – you planned for this output.

For example, in one output you may want one video and two audios, in another output you may want one captions, and in a third output you may want just one captions.

See [ERROR] BAD/MISSING LINK TEXT, [ERROR] BAD/MISSING LINK TEXT, and [ERROR] BAD/MISSING LINK TEXT for information on the fields in each type of encode.

Settings for an HLS Output

Output Settings Section

- Complete the Name modifier and Segment modifier fields as described in [ERROR] BAD/MISSING LINK TEXT.

- Set HLS Settings field as appropriate:

  - If this output is a regular output with video and audio encodes, then choose Standard HLS. More fields appear. Leave Audio Rendition Sets as is (the value is ignored), and complete the fields under M3U8 as desired; the default value is often desireable. For details on a field, choose the Info link next to the field.

  - If this output is an output that contains only a video encode and the output is part of an output group that includes an audio rendition group, then choose Standard HLS. More fields appear. Complete Audio Renditon Sets as required. complete the fields under M3U8 as desired; the default value is often desireable. For details on a field, choose the Info link next to the field.

  - If this output is an output that contains only an audio encode and the output is part of an output group that includes an audio rendition group or is part of an output group that has only audio encodes (no video at all), then choose Audio only HLS. A special set of fields appear for configuring the audio. For details on a field, choose the Info link next to the field.

Streams Section

In Stream settings, decide if you need to create more encodes for this output, based on the workflow you planned. By default, each output is set up with one video encode and one audio encode. Select the appropriate Add button or Delete button to set up the output with the encodes – video, audio, captions – you planned for this output.

For example, in one output you may want one video and two audios, in another output you may want one captions, and in a third output you may want just one captions.

See [ERROR] BAD/MISSING LINK TEXT, [ERROR] BAD/MISSING LINK TEXT, and [ERROR] BAD/MISSING LINK TEXT for information on the fields in each type of encode.

Settings for a Microsoft Smooth Output

Output Settings Section

Complete the Name modifier field as described in [ERROR] BAD/MISSING LINK TEXT.

Streams Section

In the Stream settings section, decide if you need to create more encodes for this output, based on the workflow you planned. By default, each output is set up with one video encode and one audio encode. Select the appropriate Add button or Delete button to set up the output with the encodes – video, audio, captions – you planned for this output.

For example, in one output you may want one video and two audios, in another output you may want one captions, and in a third output you may want just one captions.

See [ERROR] BAD/MISSING LINK TEXT, [ERROR] BAD/MISSING LINK TEXT, and [ERROR] BAD/MISS-ING LINK TEXT for information on the fields in each type of encode.

Settings for a UDP Output

Output Settings Section

1. Choose a value for FEC Output Settings.

2. In the fields under Network Settings, change any values as desired. For details on a field, choose the Info link next to the field.

3. In the fields under PID settings, change any values as desired. For details on a field, choose the Info link next to the field.

Streams Section

In Stream settings, decide if you need to create more encodes for this output, based on the workflow you planned. By default, each output is set up with one video encode and one audio encode. Select the appropriate Add button or Delete button to set up the output with the encodes – video, audio, captions – you planned for this output.

For example, in one output you may want one video and two audios, in another output you may want one captions, and in a third output you may want just one captions.

See [ERROR] BAD/MISSING LINK TEXT, [ERROR] BAD/MISSING LINK TEXT, and [ERROR] BAD/MISS-ING LINK TEXTfor information on the fields in each type of encode.

Step 6: Set up the Video Encode

The output section for every type of output group (Archive, HLS, Microsoft Smooth, and UDP) contains a Stream settings section. In the Stream settings section, you create "encodes" for the video, audio, and captions in the output and specify the details of how you want these assets encoded.

This section describes how to set up a video encode and assumes you have created the output that will hold the video. Note that the configuration options for a video encode are identical for all output group types.

1. In the Create channel navigation panel, find the output group (which you have already created).

2. Under that output group, find the output (which you have already created) where you want to set up a video encode.

3. Choose the link for the video encode. The fields for video encoding appear. Complete each field as appropriate. For details on a field, choose the Info link next to the field.

4. Continue setting up the audio encodes, video encodes, and captions encodes for all outputs in all output groups. When done, go to save the channel.

Step 7: Set up the Audio Encodes

The output section for every type of output group (Archive, HLS, Microsoft Smooth, and UDP) contains a Stream settings section. In the Stream settings section, you create "encodes" for the video, audio, and captions in the output and specify the details of how you want these assets encoded.

This section describes how to set up an audio encode and assumes you have created the output that will hold the audio. Note that the configuration options for an audio encode are identical for all output group types.

1. In the Create channel navigation panel, find the output group (which you have already created).

2. Under that output group, find the output (which you have already created) where you want to set up the audio encode.

3. Choose the link for one of the audio encodes (you may have created more than one encode).

4. In the Codec settings field, choose the codec to use to encode this audio asset. The remaining fields change to match this codec.

5. Complete each field as appropriate. For details on a field, choose the Info link next to the field.

6. Complete the fields in the Remix settings section if desired, or leave the defaults (to omit remixing).

7. Complete the fields in the Audio normalization settings section if desired, or leave the defaults (to omit normalization).

8. Repeat for each audio encode in this output, if any.

9. Continue setting up the audio encodes, video encodes, and captions encodes for all outputs in all output groups. When done, go to save the channel.

Step 8: Set up the Captions Encodes

The output section for every type of output group (Archive, HLS, Microsoft Smooth, and UDP) contains a Stream settings section. In the Stream settings section, you create "encodes" for the video, audio, and captions in the output and specify the details of how you want these assets encoded.

Before setting up captions, see [ERROR] BAD/MISSING LINK TEXT. There are rules about:

1. What caption formats can be generated, depending on the format of the input captions and container. For example, ARIB can only be generated from ARIB input captions, which can only appear in a TS input.

2. What caption type (embedded, object, sidecar) apply to which caption format. For example, DVB-Sub is an object type of format.

3. Which format can be included in which type of output asset. For example, HLS can take Web-VTT (a sidecar type), 608 (embedded) and burn-in.

For detailed information on setting up captions, see [ERROR] BAD/MISSING LINK TEXT.

Continue setting up the audio encodes, video encodes, and captions encodes for all outputs in all output groups. When done, go to save the channel.

Step 9: Save

You can save the channel only when you have configured and created everything you require. As soon as you save, the configuration of the channel is validated and messages are displayed for any errors. You cannot save a draft and you cannot save a channel that contains error messages.

At the bottom of the navigation pane, choose Create Channel.

The Channel panel reappears and shows the newly created channel in the list of channels. The State changes to Creating, then Ready.

Creating a Channel from a Template or by Cloning

A channel contains the details that instruct AWS Elemental MediaLive how to transcode (decode and encode) and package your input into specific outputs.

To create a channel you must provide details about inputs, about one or more output groups and their destinations, about the outputs in each output group, and about the video, audio and caption encodes in each output.

There are three ways to create a channel:

- **From scratch.** The Create form contains some fields that display system defaults and contains other fields that are empty. You can modify system defaults and complete empty fields as desired. See [ERROR] BAD/MISSING LINK TEXT.

- **Using a built-in template or custom template.** See below.

- **By cloning an existing channel. **See below.

The following procedures assume that you are familiar with all the steps in creating a channel from scratch. See [ERROR] BAD/MISSING LINK TEXT.

About Templates and Clones

About Built-in Templates

AWS Elemental MediaLive includes built-in templates. Each template is displayed in the console list with a name and description. Each template includes data for output groups and outputs, and most importantly, for encoding video to meet specific use cases (as specified in the template description).

When you use a built-in template, all sections of the **Create channel** page are populated with data except for the inputs and output destinations sections.

You can modify existing fields and complete empty fields as desired.

About Custom Templates

You or another person in your organization may have created custom templates. See [ERROR] BAD/MISSING LINK TEXT. A template may contain nearly all the data required to create a complete channel, or it may contain only portions of the data.

You need to obtain the templates you need and put them in a folder on the computer where you are working on the AWS Elemental MediaLive console. This folder is the "custom template location". You perform this task in your computer's filesystem.

When you use a custom template, all sections of the **Create channel** page are populated with data from the JSON file, except for the input data: even if the template includes input data, that data will not be pulled into the **Create channel** page.

You can modify existing fields and complete empty fields as desired.

About Cloning

Cloning lets you use an existing channel as the template for a new channel.

When you clone an existing channel, all sections of the **Create channel** page are populated with the data from the cloned channel, except for the input data, which is always left blank.

You can modify existing fields and complete empty fields as desired.

Creating a Channel from a Template

1. On the console, choose Channels in the navigation pane.

2. In the content pane, choose **Create channel**. The **Create channel** page appears.

3. In the **Channel and input details** pane, in **Channel template**, do one of the following:

   - To use a built-in template: In **Template**, choose a template from the top part of the drop-down list.

   - To clone an existing channel: In **Template**, choose a template from the bottom part of the drop-down list.

   - To use a custom template: Choose **Select custom template**. A web browser dialog appears. Navigate to the "custom template location" and select a template (a JSON file). See [ERROR] BAD/MISSING LINK TEXT for details on the custom template location.

4. Complete the fields, such as the input fields, that must always be completed. Change other fields as desired.

Creating a Channel by Cloning

You can clone a channel that is in the Channels list. (You can also clone a channel after choosing Create channel, see [ERROR] BAD/MISSING LINK TEXT.)

1. On the console, choose **Channels** in the navigation pane.

2. In the **Channel** page, choose the radio button beside the channel.

3. Choose **Clone**.

The **Create channel** page appears. It replicates all the data from the base channel *except* for the input sections, which are always empty.

1. Give the channel a new name and complete the input sections. Change other fields as desired.

Creating a Custom Template

You can create a custom template by exporting the data from an existing (and therefore validated) channel. The data is exported to a JSON file that you can then use with the console or with the CLI or REST API.

1. On the console, choose **Channels** in the navigation pane.

2. In the **Channel** page, select the channel name (not the radio button).

3. On the details page, choose **Create custom template**. A dialog appears. This dialog belongs to the operating system of the computer where you are working on the AWS Elemental MediaLive console. Follow the prompts to save the channel as a template. The template is a JSON file with the same name as the channel.

4. You can optionally open the file in a suitable editor and make changes: change field values, add fields, remove fields. Be careful to maintain valid JSON.

5. Finally, make the custom templates available to the users who will need them. Each user must put the templates in a folder that is accessible from the computer where the user will work on the AWS Elemental MediaLive console. This task is performed outside of AWS Elemental MediaLive.

Users of AWS Elemental MediaLive can use the template file with the console or with the CLI or REST API.

- When using with the console, all the data from the file *except* for the input data appears on the **Create channel **page.

- When using with the CLI or REST API, all the data in the file is used.

Editing and Deleting a Channel

Editing a Channel

You can edit any existing (saved) channel to change, add or delete output groups and outputs, and to change, add, or delete the video, audio, and caption encodes.

Note

You cannot use the edit feature to change the input asesociated with an existing channel. Instead, clone the channel and associate a different input.

1. On the **Channels** page, choose the radio button beside the channel.

2. Choose **Edit**. The Edit channel page appears. The details on this page are identical to those in Create channel. For information on working with this page, see [ERROR] BAD/MISSING LINK TEXT.

Deleting a Channel

You can delete a non-running channel from the **Channels** list or the details view.

1. On the **Channels** page, choose the radio button beside the channel.

2. If the channel is running, choose **Stop**.

3. Choose **Delete**.

Working with Captions

You can set up AWS Elemental MediaLive to include captions when it ingests the source (either captions present inside the video source or captions from an external file) and include those captions in the output in either the same or a different format. You can include several captions in the output. For example, you can include captions for several languages. You can take a source captions asset and convert it to one format in one output and another format in a different output.

You perform the setup for captions in your AWS Elemental MediaLive channel.

By default, AWS Elemental MediaLive does not ingest any captions (not even captions that are embedded in the video); you must explicitly identify the captions to ingest and the captions to output.

Note
The information in this captions section assumes that you are familiar with the general steps for creating a channel, as described in [ERROR] BAD/MISSING LINK TEXT. It also assumes that you have started creating a channel, including associating an input with the channel.

Supported Features

Supported Formats

AWS Elemental MediaLive supports specific formats in inputs and specific formats in outputs. See [ERROR] BAD/MISSING LINK TEXT for a table that lists the supported captions formats, with a reference to the standard that defines that format. This table specifies whether the format is supported as input or output or both.

Format Support by Output Container

- The type of input container. A given input container can contain captions in some formats and not in others.

- The format of the input captions. A given format of captions can be converted to some formats and not to others.

- The type of output containers. A given output container supports some caption formats and not others.

For more information, see [ERROR] BAD/MISSING LINK TEXT.

Supported Captions Categories

Different formats are grouped into the same category. For example, TTML and WebVTT are grouped in the "sidecar" category. AWS Elemental MediaLive supports several categories of captions. The main ones are the following:

- Embedded. The captions are carried inside the video encode.

- Captions Object. The captions are in their own "captions encode." They are not part of the video encode. But they are in the same output as their corresponding video and audio encodes.

- Sidecar. The captions are each in their own output, separate from the output that contains the video and audio. There can be several "captions-only" outputs, for example, one for each desired language.

You need to be aware of captions categories when you set up captions in the output. For more information about all categories and which category each captions format belongs to, see [ERROR] BAD/MISSING LINK TEXT.

Support for Languages

If the source includes captions in multiple languages, you can include multiple languages in the output as follows:

- **Embedded-to-Embedded.** For any of the embedded source formats, if you are doing "embedded in, embedded out" (also known as embedded-to-embedded), all languages that are in the input are included in the output. You can't remove any of the languages.

- **Embedded In, Other Out.** For any of the embedded source formats, if you are doing "embedded in, other out," you can specify which languages to extract and include in an output.

- **Teletext-to-Teletext.** For teletext source, if you are doing "teletext in, teletext out" (also known as teletext-to-teletext), all languages (pages) are included in the output. You can't strip out any languages. In fact, the entire teletext content is included in the output; you can't strip out any of the pages. Furthermore, teletext-to-teletext is supported only in TS outputs.

- **Teletext In, Other Out.** For teletext source, if you are doing "teletext in, other out," you can specify which languages to extract and which languages to include in an output.

- **Any Other Combination.** For all other sources, you always specify the language to extract from the input and the language to include in an output, regardless of the source format and output format.

Support for Font Styles in Output Captions

Depending on the scenario, you can specify the style for fonts, including color, outline, and background color.

Font Style Options

Source Caption	Output Caption	Options for Font Style
ARIB	ARIB	None. The font styles in the input are automatically passed through in the output.
SCTE-27	SCTE-27	None. The font styles in the input are automatically passed through in the output.
DVB-Sub	DVB-Sub	None. The font styles in the input are automatically passed through in the output.
Teletext	Teletext	None. The font styles in the input are automatically passed through in the output.
Any Supported Caption	Burn-in	You can specify font styles in the output. If you don't specify styles, the AWS Elemental MediaLive defaults are used.
Any Supported Caption	DVB-Sub	You can specify font styles in the output. If you don't specify styles, the AWS Elemental MediaLive defaults are used.
An Embedded Combination (Embedded, Embedded+SCTE-20, SCTE-20+Embedded)	TTML	The font information in the source can be copied to the output, or you can let the downstream player determine the font style.
Teletext	TTML	The font information in the source can be copied to the output, or you can let the downstream player determine the font style.
Any Other	Any Other	No control: the font style is always determined by the downstream player.

Typical Scenarios

- Use Case: One Input Format to One Output and Not Converted
- Use Case: One Input Format Converted to One Different Format in One Output
- Use Case: One Input Format Converted to Different Formats, One Format for Each Output
- Use Case: One Captions Output Shared by Multiple Video Encodes

Use Case: One Input Format to One Output and Not Converted

The input is set up with one format of captions and two or more languages. You want to maintain the format in the output. You want to produce only one type of output and include all the languages in that output.

For example, the input has embedded captions in English and French. You want to produce HLS output that includes embedded captions in both English and French.

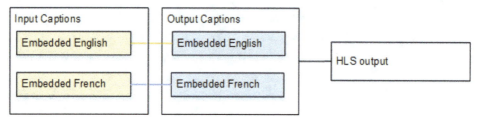

Use Case: One Input Format Converted to One Different Format in One Output

The input is set up with one format of captions and two or more languages. You want to convert the captions to a different format in the output. You want to produce only one type of output and include all the languages in that output.

For example, the input has embedded captions in German and French. You want to convert the captions to DVB-Sub and include these captions in both languages in a UDP output.

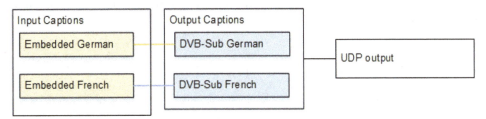

Use Case: One Input Format Converted to Different Formats, One Format for Each Output

This example shows how to implement the third use casefrom the typical scenarios. The input is set up with one format of captions and two or more languages. You want to produce several different types of output. In each output, you want to convert the captions to a different format but include all the languages.

For example, the input has teletext captions in Czech and Polish. You want to produce a Microsoft Smooth output and an HLS output. In the Microsoft Smooth output, you want to include one video and one audio and you want to convert the captions to TTML. In the HLS output, you want to include one video and one audio and you want to convert the captions to WebVTT.

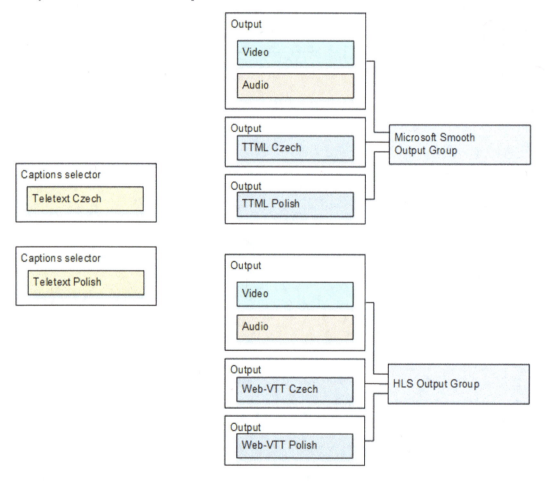

Setup

1. In the channel that you are creating, in the navigation pane, choose **Channel and input details**.

2. Choose **Add caption selector** twice to create the following caption selectors:

   - Caption selector 1 for Teletext Czech. Specify the page that holds the Czech captions.

   - Caption selector 2 for Teletext Polish. Specify the page that holds the Polish captions.

   Although you are including the captions in two different outputs (Microsoft Smooth and HLS), you need to extract them from the input only once, so you need to create only one caption selector for each language.

3. Create a Microsoft Smooth output group and configure it as follows:

1. Create one output and set up the video and audio.

2. Create a second output that contains one captions encode and no video or audio encodes, and with the following settings:

   - **Caption selector name**: Caption Selector 1.

   - **Captions settings**: TTML.

   - **Language code** and **Language description**: Czech.

   - **Style control**: Set as desired.

3. Create a third output that contains one captions encode and no video or audio encodes, with the following settings:

   - **Caption selector name**: Caption Selector 2.

   - **Captions settings**: TTML.

   - **Language code** and **Language description**: Polish.

   - Other fields: same as the second output (the Czech captions).

4. Create an HLS output group and configure it as follows:

   1. Create one output and set up the video and audio.

   2. Create a second output that contains one captions encode and no video or audio encodes, and with the following settings:

      - **Caption selector name**: Caption Selector 1.

      - **Captions settings**: WebVTT.

      - **Language code** and **Language description**: Czech.

      - Other fields: Set as desired.

   3. Create a third caption output that contains one captions encode and no video or audio encodes, and with the following settings:

      - **Caption selector name**: Caption Selector 2.

      - **Captions settings**: WebVTT

      - **Language code** and **Language description**: Polish.

      - Other fields: same as the second output (the Czech captions).

5. Finish setting up the channel and save it.

Use Case: One Captions Output Shared by Multiple Video Encodes

This example shows how to set up captions in an ABR workflow. The first setup shows how to set up an ABR workflow when the captions are in the same output as the video, meaning that the captions are either embedded or captions style.

The second setup shows how to set up an ABR workflow when the captions belong to the sidecar category, in which case each captions is in its own output.

Setup with Embedded or Object-style Captions

This example shows how to implement the fourth use case from the typical scenarios. For example, you want to produce an HLS output with three video encodes (one for low-resolution video, one for medium, one for high) and one audio. You also want to include embedded captions (in English and Spanish) and associate them with all three video encodes.

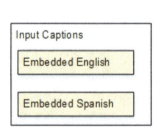

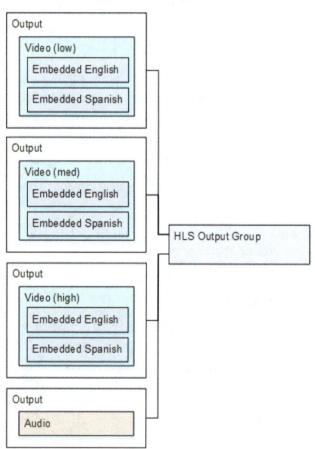

1. In the channel that you are creating, in the navigation pane, choose **Channel and input details**.

2. Choose **Add caption selector** to create one caption selector. Set **Selector settings** to **Embedded source**.

3. Create an HLS output group.

4. Create one output and set up the video and audio for low-resolution video.

5. In that same output, create one captions asset with the following:

   - **Caption selector name**: Caption selector 1.

- **Caption settings**: One of the Embedded formats.
- **Language code** and **Language description**: Leave blank; with embedded-to-embedded captions, all the languages are included.

6. Create a second output and set up the video and audio for medium-resolution video.

7. In that same output, create one captions asset with the following:

- **Caption selector name**: Caption selector 1.
- **Caption settings**: One of the Embedded formats.
- **Language code** and **Language description**: Leave blank; with embedded captions, all the languages are included.

8. Create a third output and set up the video and audio for high-resolution video.

9. In that same output, create one captions asset with the following:

- **Caption selector name**: Caption selector 1.
- **Caption settings**: One of the Embedded formats.
- **Language code** and **Language description**: Leave blank; with embedded captions, all the languages are included.

10. Finish setting up the channel and save it.

Setup with Sidecar Captions

This example shows an ABR workflow where the captions are in sidecars. For example, you want to produce a Microsoft Smooth output with three video encodes (one for low-resolution video, one for medium, one for high) and one audio. These encodes are in a Microsoft Smooth output. You want to ingest embedded captions (in English and Spanish) and convert them to TTML captions, one for English and one for Spanish.

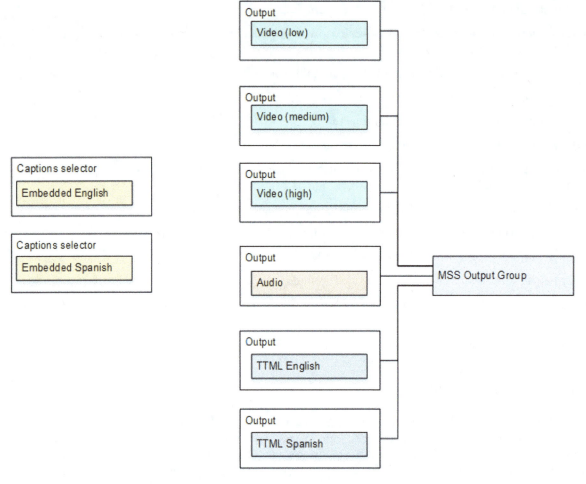

1. In the channel that you are creating, in the navigation pane, choose **Channel and input details**.

2. Choose **Add caption selector** twice to create the following caption selectors:

   - Caption selector 1: for Embedded English.

   - Caption Selector 2: for Embedded Spanish.

3. Create a Microsoft Smooth output group.

4. Create one output that contains one video encode and set it up for low-resolution video.

5. Create a second output that contains one video encode and set it up for medium-resolution video.

6. Create a third output that contains one video encode and set it up for high-resolution video.

7. Create a fourth output that contains one audio encode and no video encode.

8. Create a fifth output that contains one captions encode and no video or audio encodes, and with the following settings for the captions encode:

   - **Caption selector name**: Caption selector 1.

   - **Caption settings**: TTML.

   - **Language code** and **Language description**: English.

9. Create a sixth output that contains one captions encode and no video or audio encodes, and with the following settings for the captions encode:

   - **Caption selector name**: Caption selector 2.

- **Caption settings**: TTML.

- **Language code** and **Language description**: Spanish.

10. Finish setting up the channel and save it.

Setting Up for Captions

When you create a channel, you must specify the format of the input captions, then specify the desired format of the captions for every output. When you save the channel, your choices are validated according to the supported combinations of input container, source caption, and output container.

- Step 1: Create Caption Selectors in the Input
- Step 2: Plan Captions for the Outputs
- Step 3: Match Formats to Categories
- Step 4: Create Captions Encodes

Step 1: Create Caption Selectors in the Input

You must identify the captions that you want to use and assign each to a caption selector. If you don't create any caption selectors, you will not be able to include captions in the output. All the captions will be removed from the media.

Identify the Captions You Want

1. Identify which captions are in the input (the provider of the input should provide you with this information) and identify which captions are available to you as external files. Identify the caption formats and, for each format, the languages.

2. Identify which of those formats and languages that you want to use.

3. Determine how many caption selectors to create in the input in the channel, using the following guidance:

   - For embedded-to-embedded, create a single caption selector for all languages. All languages are passed through; there is no other option. For details, see [ERROR] BAD/MISSING LINK TEXT.

   - For teletext-to-teletext, create a single caption selector for all languages (in fact, one caption selector for the entire content). All languages are passed through; there is no other option. For details, see [ERROR] BAD/MISSING LINK TEXT.

   - In all other cases, create one caption selector for each language and format combination.

You end up with a list of caption selectors to create. For example:

- Caption Selector 1: Teletext captions in Czech
- Caption Selector 2: Teletext captions in Polish

Create Caption Selectors

In AWS Elemental MediaLive, extract the desired captions by adding a caption selector in the channel. Each extracted caption is contained in one caption selector.

1. In the channel that you are creating, in the navigation pane, choose **Channel and input details**.

2. For **Input settings**, choose **Add caption selectors**.

3. For **Caption selector name**, type a suitable name. For example, TTML Czech.

4. For **Selector settings**, choose the format of the source captions.

5. For most formats, more fields appear. For details about a field, choose the Info link next to the field. In addition, see extra information on DVB-Sub or SCTE-27, on Embedded, or on Teletext.

6. Create more caption selectors, as required.

Information for DVB-Sub or SCTE-27

DVB-Sub and SCTE-27 formats are supported only in TS inputs. You must specify the location of the captions by completing the PID and/or Language code fields in one of these ways.

PID	Language Code	Result
Specified	Blank	Extracts captions from the specified PID.
Blank	Specified	Extracts the specified language, whichever PID that happens to be in.
Specified	Specified	Extracts captions from that PID; the language is informational.
Blank	Blank	Valid only if the source is DVB-Sub and the output is DVB-Sub. With this combination of PID and Language, all input DVB-Sub PIDs will be included in the output.Not valid for SCTE-27.

Information for Embedded

Read this section if the input captions are any of the following: embedded (EIA-608 or CEA-708), embedded+SCTE-20, SCTE-20+embedded, or SCTE-20.

How Many Caption Selectors?

- If you are doing embedded-to-embedded, create only one caption selector, even if you want to include multiple languages in the output. With this scenario, all languages are automatically extracted and are automatically included in the output.

- If you are doing embedded-to-other, create one caption selector for each language that you want to include in the output, to a maximum of four selectors.

- If you are doing embedded-to-embedded in some outputs and embedded-to-other in other outputs, create one caption selector for the embedded-to-embedded, then create up to four more selectors for the embedded-to-other, one for each desired language.

Caption Selector Fields

- **Selector settings**:

  - Choose embedded if the source captions are embedded (EIA-608 or CEA-708), embedded+SCTE-20, or SCTE-20+embedded.

  - Choose SCTE-20 if the source captions are SCTE-20 alone.

- **EIA-608 track number**: This field specifies the language to extract. Complete as follows:

  - If you are doing embedded-to-embedded captions (you are creating only one caption selector for the input embedded captions), this field is ignored, so keep the default.

  - If you are converting embedded to another format, (you are creating several caption selectors, one for each language), specify the number of the CC instance (from the input) that holds the desired language.

- **Convert 608 to 708**: The embedded source captions can be EIA-608 captions, CEA-708 captions, or both EIA-608 and CEA-708. You can specify how you want these captions to be handled when AWS Elemental MediaLive is ingesting content. The following table describes the behavior for various scenarios. [See the AWS documentation website for more details]

- **SCTE-20 detection**: If the source captions combine embedded (EIA-608 or CEA-708) and SCTE-20, you might want to set this field to Auto. AWS Elemental MediaLive will give preference to the 608/708 embedded captions but will switch to use the SCTE-20 captions when necessary. If you set this field to Off, AWS Elemental MediaLive will never use the SCTE-20 captions.

Information for Teletext

Teletext is a form of data that can contain several types of information, not just captions. Teletext can be present in TS input, in which case it might be referred to as "DVB Teletext." Teletext can be handled in one of the following ways:

- If you want to include the entire teletext input, you must do teletext-to-teletext. The entire teletext can never be converted to another format. Teletext-to-teletext is supported only in a TS output.

- Individual captions pages (the captions in a specific language) can be extracted and converted to another captions format.

- Individual captions pages (the captions in a specific language) *cannot* be extracted and kept in teletext. If you want to extract individual captions pages, you must convert them to another format.

How Many Caption Selectors?

- If you are doing teletext-to-teletext captions, create only one caption selector, even if you want to include multiple languages in the output. With this scenario, all languages are automatically extracted and are automatically included in the output.

- If you are doing teletext-to-other, create one caption selector for each language that you want to include in the output. For example, one selector to extract English teletext, and one selector to extract Swedish teletext.

- If you are doing teletext-to-teletext in some outputs and teletext-to-other in other outputs, create one caption selector for the teletext-to-teletext, and then create individual selectors for the teletext-to-other, one for each language being converted.

Caption Selector Fields

- **Selector settings**: Choose **Teletext**.

- **Page number**: This field specifies the page of the desired language. Complete as follows:

  - If you are doing teletext-to-teletext captions (you are creating only one caption selector for the input captions), leave blank: the value is ignored.

  - If you are converting teletext to another format (you are creating several caption selectors, one for each language), specify the page for the desired language. If you leave this field blank, you will get a validation error when you save the channel.

Step 2: Plan Captions for the Outputs

If you followed the instructions in [ERROR] BAD/MISSING LINK TEXT, you should have a list of the caption formats and languages that will be available for inclusion in the outputs.

You must now plan the caption information for the outputs:

1. Identify the types of output media that you plan to create in the channel. For example, Microsoft Smooth and HLS.

2. Identify the combinations of video and audio that you plan to create for each output media.

3. For each output media, identify which input captions will be converted to which output formats. For example, you will convert teletext captions to TTML for the Microsoft Smooth output media, and those same teletext captions to Web-VTT for the HLS output media.

   The output formats that are possible depend on the input formats and the type of output media. See [ERROR] BAD/MISSING LINK TEXT to determine which output captions are possible given the input format.

4. Identify the languages for each output format:

   - In general, count each language separately.

   - Exception: For embedded-to-embedded, count all languages as one.

   - Exception: For teletext-to-teletext, count all languages as one.

The Result

You end up with a list of outputs, and the captions formats and languages for each output. For example:

- Microsoft Smooth output with TTML captions in Czech

- Microsoft Smooth output with TTML captions in Polish

- HLS output with Web-VTT captions in Czech

- HLS output with Web-VTT captions in Polish

Outputting Multiple Formats

You can include captions from two or more different formats in an output. For example, you can include both embedded captions and WebVTT captions in an HLS output, to give the downstream system more choices about which captions to use. The only rules for multiple formats are the following:

- The output container must support all the formats. See [ERROR] BAD/MISSING LINK TEXT.

- The font styles in all the captions that are associated with an output must match. This means that the end result must be identical, not that you must use the same option to get that result. For example, all captions that are associated with the output must be white for the first language and blue for the second language.

Managing this style matching can be a little tricky. For information about the font style options, see Support for Font Styles in Output Captions.

Step 3: Match Formats to Categories

There are different procedures to follow to create caption encodes in the output. The correct procedure depends on the "category" that of the output captions belongs to . There are five categories of captions, described in the following table.

On the list of outputs that you have created, make a note of the category that each captions option belongs to.

Captions Format	Category of This Format
ARIB	Object
Burn-in	Burn-in
DVB-Sub	Object
Embedded	Embedded
Embedded+SCTE-20	Embedded
SCTE-20+Embedded	Embedded
SCTE-27	Object
SMPTE-TT	Stream in Microsoft Smooth
Teletext	Object
TTML	Sidecar
WebVTT	Sidecar

For example, your list of outputs might now look like this:

- Microsoft Smooth output with TTML captions (sidecar) in Czech.

- Microsoft Smooth output with TTML captions (sidecar) in Polish.

- HLS output with Web-VTT captions (sidecar) in Czech.

- HLS output with Web-VTT captions (sidecar) in Polish.

Embedded in Video

The captions are carried inside the video encode, which is itself in an output in the output group. There is only ever one captions asset within that video encode, although that asset might contain captions for several languages.

Captions Object

The captions are in their own "captions encode" in an output in the output group. They are not part of the video encode. However, they are in the same output as their corresponding video and audio encodes. There might be several captions encodes in the output, for example, for different languages.

Sidecar

The captions are each in their own output in the output group, separate from the output that contains the video and audio. Each captions output contains only one captions asset (file). The output group might contain several "captions-only" outputs, for example, one for each language in the output group.

SMPTE-TT in Microsoft Smooth

The captions are handled as a separate stream in Microsoft Smooth.

Burn-in

The captions are converted into text and then overlaid on the picture directly in the video encode. Strictly speaking, once the overlay occurs, these are not really captions because they are indistinguishable from the video.

Step 4: Create Captions Encodes

Go through the list of outputs you created and set up the captions in each output group, one by one.

Follow the procedure that applies to the format category of the captions output:

- [ERROR] BAD/MISSING LINK TEXT.
- [ERROR] BAD/MISSING LINK TEXT.
- [ERROR] BAD/MISSING LINK TEXT.

All Captions except Sidecar or SMPTE-TT in Microsoft Smooth

Follow this procedure if the format of the captions asset that you want to add belongs to the category of embedded, burn-in, or object.

1. In the channel that you are creating, in the navigation pane, find the output group (which you have already created). For example, find the HLS output group.

2. Find the output where you want to add the captions, or create a new output. This output might already be set up with video and audio, or you could set up the video and audio after setting up the captions.

3. Choose the output.

4. For **Stream settings**, choose **Add caption**.

5. For **Caption description name**, type a name for this captions asset that is unique in the channel. For example, Embedded. Or accept the default (which is autogenerated).

6. For **Caption selector name**, type the name of the caption selector that you created in step 1. Specify the selector that identifies the captions asset that is the source for the captions in this output.

7. For **Caption settings**, choose the captions format for the output captions.

8. Complete the fields that appear for the selected format. For details about a field, choose the Info link beside the field. For tips about font styles in DVB-Sub or burn-in, see Font Styles for Burn-in or DVB-Sub Output.

9. If the output format is embedded and the output group is HLS, you can include caption language information in the manifest. You perform this setup in the output settings (separate from the captions encode). See HLS manifest .

10. If the output format is ARIB or DVB-Sub or SCTE-27, you must perform some extra setup in the output settings (separate from the captions encode). See PIDS for ARIB output or PIDs for DVB-Sub output or PIDs for SCTE-27 or PIDs for Teletext output.

11. Repeat these steps to create captions in more outputs and output groups, as applicable.

Sidecar Captions

Follow this procedure if the format of the captions asset that you want to add is a sidecar, as identified in [ERROR] BAD/MISSING LINK TEXT.

1. In the channel that you are creating, in the navigation pane, find the output group (which you have already created). For example, find the HLS output group.

2. Find the output where you want to add the captions, or create a new output. This output might already be set up with video and audio, or you could set up the video and audio after setting up the captions.

3. Choose the output.

4. For **Stream settings**, remove the video and audio encodes from this output by choosing the encode and selecting **Remove video** or **Remove audio**.

5. Choose **Add caption**. This output should now contain one caption section and no video or audio sections.

6. For **Caption description name**, type a name for this captions asset that is unique in the channel. For example, webvtt Czech. Or accept the default (which is autogenerated).

7. For **Caption selector name**, type the name of the caption selector that you created in step 1. Specify the selector that identifies the captions asset that is the source for the captions in this output.

8. For **Caption settings**, choose the sidecar format for the output captions.

9. Complete the fields that appear for the selected format. For details about a field, choose the Info link beside the field.

10. Repeat these steps to create sidecar captions in this or another output group, as applicable.

SMPTE-TT Captions in Microsoft Smooth

Follow this procedure to add output captions in the SMPTE-TT format (only possible in a Microsoft Smooth output group).

1. In the channel that you are creating, in the navigation pane, find the Microsoft Smooth output group (which you have already created).

2. Find the output where you want to add the captions, or create a new output. This output might already be set up with video and audio, or you could set up the video and audio after setting up the captions.

3. Choose the output.

4. For **Stream settings**, remove the video and audio encodes from this output by choosing the encode and selecting **Remove video** or **Remove audio**.

5. Choose **Add caption**. This output should now contain one caption section and no video or audio sections.

6. For **Caption description name**, type a name for this captions asset that is unique in the channel. For example, SmpteTT Czech. Or accept the default (which is autogenerated).

7. For **Caption selector name**, type the name of the caption selector that you created in step 1. Specify the selector that identifies the captions asset that is the source for the captions in this output.

8. For **Caption settings**, choose SMPTE-TT.

9. Complete the fields that appear for the selected format. For details about a field, choose the Info link beside the field.

10. Repeat these steps to create more SMPTE-TT captions in the Microsoft Smooth output group, as applicable.

Font Styles for Burn-in or DVB-Sub

You can specify the look of the captions if the output captions are Burn-in or DVB-Sub.

If you are using the same caption source in several outputs and both those outputs use the same format, then you must set up the font style information identically in each output. If you do not, you will get an error when you save the channel.

For example, output A might use Caption Selector 1 with the Destination Type set to Burn-in. And output B might also use Caption Selector 1 with the Destination Type set to Burn-in. You set the font information once in output 1 and again in output 2. But you must make sure to set up all the font information identically in both outputs.

Complete the PIDs for ARIB

Complete this step if the output group is UDP/TS and the output caption is ARIB.

1. In the relevant UDP output group, choose the output that has the ARIB captions.

2. For **PID settings**, complete **ARIB captions PID control **and **ARIB captions PID** as follows:

3.

[See the AWS documentation website for more details]

Complete the PIDs for DVB-Sub

Complete this step if the output group is UDP and the output caption is DVB-Sub.

1. In the relevant UDP output group, choose the output that has the DVB-Sub captions.

2. For **PID settings**, in **DVB-Sub PIDs**, type the PID for the DVB-Sub caption in this output. Or keep the default.

Complete the PIDs for SCTE-27

Complete this step if the output group is UDP and the output caption is SCTE-27.

1. In the relevant UDP output group, choose the output that has the SCTE-27 captions.

2. For **PID settings**, in **SCTE-27 PIDs**, type the PID for the SCTE-27 caption in this output. Or keep the default.

Complete the PIDs for Teletext

Complete this step if the output group is UDP and the output caption is Teletext.

1. In the relevant UDP output group, choose the output that has the Teletext captions.

2. For **PID settings**, in **DVB teletext PID**, type the PID for the Teletext captions in this output. Or keep the default.

Set up the HLS Manifest

If the captions are embedded captions and the output is HLS, you can choose to include caption language information in the manifest.

1. In the HLS output group, for **Captions**, in **Caption language setting**, choose **Insert**. Choosing this option inserts lines in the manifest for each embedded captions language. It inserts as many lines as the mappings that you will add in the next step.

2. For **HLS settings**, in **Caption language mappings**, choose **Add caption language mappings**.

3. Choose **Add caption language mappings** to add more groups, one for each embedded captions asset, to a maximum of four groups.

4. Complete each group to identify the CC (caption channel) number and its language. For example, if caption channel 1 is French, then set up the three fields with "1", "FRE", and "French".

    The order in which you enter the languages must match the order of the captions in the source. For example, if the captions are in the order French, then English, then Spanish, then Portuguese, then set up CC1 as French, CC2 as English, and so on. If you do not order them correctly, the captions in the manifest will be tagged with the wrong languages.

Examples

The following examples describe how to implement the use cases from [ERROR] BAD/MISSING LINK TEXT.

Use Case: One Input Format to One Output

This example shows how to implement the first use case from the typical scenarios. The input is set up with one format of captions and two or more languages. You want to maintain the format in the output. You want to produce only one type of output and include all the languages in that output.

For example, the input has embedded captions in English and French. You want to produce an HLS output that includes embedded captions in both English and French, plus one video and one audio.

This example illustrates two important features of an embedded-to-embedded workflow. First, you do not create separate caption selectors; all of the languages are all automatically included. Second, if you are outputting to HLS, there is an opportunity to specify the languages and the order in which they appear.

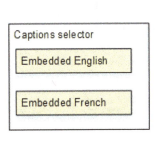
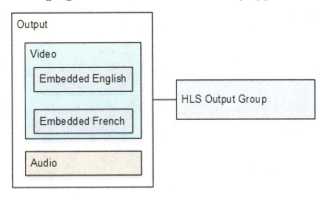

Setup

1. In the channel that you are creating, in the navigation pane, choose **Channel and input details**.

2. For **Input settings**, choose **Add caption selector** to create one caption selector. Set **Selector settings** to **Embedded source**.

3. Create an HLS output group.

4. Create one output and set up the video and audio.

5. In that same output, create one captions asset with the following:

   - **Caption selector name**: Caption selector 1.

   - **Caption settings**: One of the Embedded formats.

   - **Language code** and **Language description**: Leave blank; with embedded captions, all the languages are included.

6. In the HLS output group, in **Captions**, in **Caption language setting**, choose **Insert**.

7. For **HLS settings**, in **Caption language mappings**, choose **Add caption language mappings** twice (once for each language).

8. Complete the first group of mapping fields with ”1,” ”ENG,” and ”English” and the second group with ”2,” ”FRE,” and ”French.”

9. Finish setting up the channel and save it.

Use Case: One Input Format Converted to One Different Output Format

This example shows how to implement the second use casefrom the typical scenarios. The input includes two captions languages, and the single output will convert those captions. For example, the input has embedded captions in German and French. You want to produce a UDP output with both captions converted to DVB-Sub, plus one video and one audio.

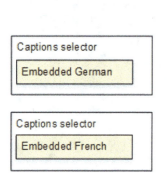
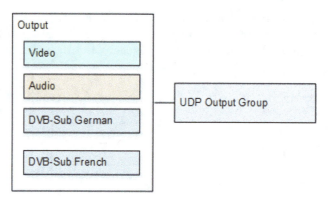

Setup

1. In the channel that you are creating, in the navigation pane, choose **Channel and input details**.

2. Choose **Add caption selector** twice, to create Caption selector 1 (for German) and Caption selector 2 (for French). In both cases, set **Selector settings** to **Embedded source**.

3. Create a UDP output group.

4. Create one output and set up the video and audio.

5. In this output, choose **Add caption** to create a caption encode.

   - **Caption selector name**: Caption selector 1.

   - **Caption settings**: DVB-Sub.

   - **Language code** and **Language description**: German.

   - Other fields: Keep the defaults or complete as desired.

6. Choose **Add caption** again to create another caption encode. Set up this encode for the French captions. Make sure that you set up the font fields for German and French in exactly the same way.

7. Finish setting up the channel and save it.

SCTE-35 Message Processing

SCTE-35 messages are messages that are embedded in the video input. These messages provide information about advertisement availability, also known as ad avail events, and other non-ad avail events.

You can include (pass through) or remove the cueing information that is conveyed by these messages in the output streams (video, audio, closed captioning, data) and any associated manifests. AWS Elemental MediaLive does not support processing of manifests that are present in the input. The information in input manifests is not ingested by AWS Elemental MediaLive or included in the output or the output manifest.

You can also blank out the video, audio, and captions within the cueing information.

To use the ad avail features of AWS Elemental MediaLive, you should be familiar with the SCTE-35 standard and optionally with the SCTE-67 standard. You should also be familiar with how the input that you are encoding implements those standards.

Note
The information in this SCTE-35 section assumes that you are familiar with the general steps for creating a channel, as described in [ERROR] BAD/MISSING LINK TEXT. It also assumes that you have started creating a channel, including associating an input with the channel.

- About Message Processing
- Getting Ready: Set the Ad Avail Mode
- Enabling Manifest Decoration
- Enabling Ad Avail Blanking
- Enabling Blackout
- SCTE-35 Passthrough or Removal
- Sample Manifests - HLS

About Message Processing

AWS Elemental MediaLive works with the SCTE-35 messages in MPEG-2 transport stream (TS) inputs. These messages might or might not include segmentation descriptors.

Processing Features

Blanking and Blackout

The "cue out" and "cue in" instructions in SCTE-35 messages line up with specific content in the video, audio, and captions streams. You can set up so that this content is blanked out in the output:

- The content for ad avails is blanked out using the ad avail blanking feature.
- The content for other messages is blanked out using the blackout feature.

The behavior you want must be set up in the channel.

For more information, see [ERROR] BAD/MISSING LINK TEXT and [ERROR] BAD/MISSING LINK TEXT.

Manifest Decoration

- HLS outputs can be set up so that their manifests include instructions that correspond to the original SCTE-35 message content. Decorate the HLS manifest with one or more of the following types of ad markers:
  - Adobe
  - Elemental
  - SCTE-35 enhanced
- Microsoft Smooth outputs can be set up so that the sparse track includes instructions that correspond to the original SCTE-35 message content.

The desired behavior must be set up in the channel. For more information, see [ERROR] BAD/MISSING LINK TEXT.

SCTE-35 Passthrough

You can include (pass through) all the SCTE-35 messages in the output data stream in any TS output. Or you can remove them.

Removing messages does not prevent you blanking or blacking out video content. The two options do not depend on each other.

The desired behavior must be set up in the channel. For more information, see [ERROR] BAD/MISSING LINK TEXT.

Blanking Compared to Passthrough and Manifest Decoration

It is important to understand that the logic for blanking ad content works on the video content associated with the ad avail event, while the logic for passthrough and manifest decoration works on the actual SCTE-35 message. The video content and the SCTE-35 message are different entities.

This means that you can blank ad avails and not pass through SCTE-35 messages, or not blank ad avails and not pass through SCTE-35 messages and decorate the manifest, or any combination. The actions are independent.

The only exception to this rule is for HLS outputs: manifest decoration and passthrough are either both enabled or both disabled.

Processing Features – Default Behavior

The default handling of SCTE-35 by AWS Elemental MediaLive is the following:

- No passthrough – Do not pass through SCTE-35 messages in any data stream outputs.
- No blanking or blackout – Do not blank out video content for any events. Leave the content as is.
- No manifest decoration – Do not convert any SCTE-35 messages to event information in any output manifests or data streams.

If this is the desired behavior, you do not need to read any further in this SCTE-35 section.

Scope of Processing by Feature

The SCTE-35 features have different scopes in terms of the output groups and outputs that they affect:

Ad avail blanking

Ad avail blanking applies at the global output level. All the ad avails in every output in every output group are blanked.

Blackout

Blackout applies at the global output level. All the relevant content in every output in every output group are blanked.

**Decoration **

Manifest decoration applies at the output group level. All the outputs in that output group have their manifests decorated.

SCTE-35 Passthrough or Removal

SCTE-35 passthrough or removal applies at the output level. The messages are passed through or removed only in a specific output.

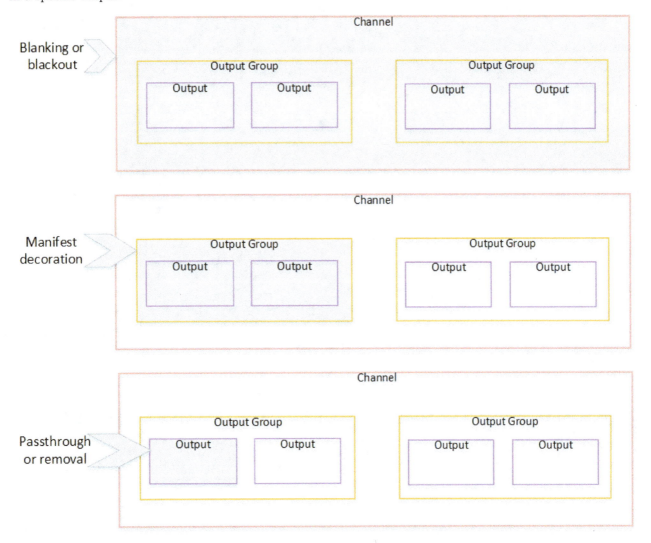

Output Types and Features

The table below summarizes which features apply to the various types of output.

Output	Passthrough in TS Outputs	Manifest Decoration	Blanking	See
Archive	Applicable	Not applicable.	Applicable	[ERROR] BAD/MISSING LINK TEXT
HLS	Applicable	Applicable	Applicable	[ERROR] BAD/MISSING LINK TEXT
Microsoft Smooth	Not applicable	Applicable	Applicable	[ERROR] BAD/MISSING LINK TEXT
UDP	Applicable	Not applicable	Applicable	[ERROR] BAD/MISSING LINK TEXT

Archive Output with MPEG-2 Container

A transport stream in an MPEG-2 container supports passthrough of the SCTE-35 messages, but it does not support creation of a manifest. Therefore, the processing options that are valid are shown in the following table.

SCTE-35 Passthrough	Manifest Decoration	Blanking and Blackout	Effect
Enabled	Not applicable	Yes or No	Turn on passthrough of SCTE-35 messages. You could also implement blanking and blackout.
Disabled	Not applicable	No	Turn off passthrough in order to remove SCTE-35 messages from the video stream. Do not implement blanking or blackout. Choose this option only if, in a downstream system, you do not want to replace video that was originally marked by cues.

HLS Output

HLS output supports both passthrough of the SCTE-35 messages and manifest decoration. In fact, with HLS outputs, passthrough and manifest decoration are either both enabled or both disabled.

Therefore, the processing options that make sense are shown in the following table.

SCTE-35 Passthrough	Manifest Decoration	Blanking and Blackout	Effect
Enabled	Enabled	Yes or No	Turn on passthrough of SCTE-35 messages and manifest decoration. You could also implement blanking and blackout.
Disabled	Disabled	No	Turn off passthrough in order to remove SCTE-35 messages from the video stream. Turn off manifest decoration. Do not implement blanking or blackout. Choose this option only if, in a downstream system, you do not want to replace video that was originally marked by cues.

Microsoft Smooth Output

Microsoft Smooth output does not support passthrough of the SCTE-35 messages, but does support instructions in the sparse track. Therefore, the processing options that make sense are:

SCTE-35 Passthrough	Manifest Decoration	Blanking and Blackout	Effect
Not applicable (SCTE-35 messages are never included in output)	Enabled	Yes or No	SCTE-35 messages are removed from the video stream. But instructions are included in the sparse track. You could also implement blanking and blackout.
Not applicable	Disabled	No	SCTE-35 messages are removed from the output. The sparse track doesn't include instructions. Don't implement blanking or blackout because without SCTE-35 messages in the video stream and without data in the sparse track, it will be impossible to find these blanks and blackouts programmatically in the output.

UDP Output

UDP output supports passthrough of the SCTE-35 messages, but it does not support creation of a manifest. Therefore, the processing options that make sense are shown in the following table.

SCTE-35 Passthrough	Manifest Decoration	Blanking and Blackout	Effect
Enabled	Not applicable	Yes or No	Turn on passthrough of SCTE-35 messages. You could also implement blanking and blackout.
Disabled	Not applicable	No	Turn off passthrough in order to remove SCTE-35 messages from the video stream. Do not implement blanking or blackout. Choose this option only if, in a downstream system, you do not want to replace video that was originally marked by cues.

Getting Ready: Set the Ad Avail Mode

Follow this procedure if you want to support one or more of the following features:

- Manifest decoration
- Ad avail blanking

If your processing does not involve at least one of these features, the ad avail mode is ignored.****

The Procedure to Set Mode

You must set the Ad Avail mode to notify AWS Elemental MediaLive of the ID type of SCTE-35 messages that the input is using to indicate ad avail events.

1. In the channel that you are creating, in the navigation pane, choose **General settings**.

2. Choose **Avail configuration**.

3. Set the **Avail settings**:

   - SCTE-35 splice insert (default): Select this mode if the input uses splice inserts to indicate ad avails. The input might also contain messages for others events such as chapters or programs.

   - SCTE-35 time signal apos: Select this mode if the input contains time signals of segmentation type **Placement opportunity**. The input might also contain messages for other events such as chapters or programs.

   The mode identifies which of all possible events are treated as triggers for ad avails and as triggers for blackouts. In turn, these triggers affect how manifests are decorated, when video is blanked, and when video is blacked out.

4. In **Ad avail offset**, set a value, if desired. See the help for this field.

5. Leave **web_delivery_allowed_flag** and **no_regional_blackout_flag** as Follow for now. For information about these fields, see [ERROR] BAD/MISSING LINK TEXT.

Enabling Manifest Decoration

You can choose to interpret SCTE-35 messages from the original input and insert corresponding instructions into the output manifest for the following outputs:

- HLS

- Microsoft Smooth (the instructions are inserted in the sparse track).

Manifest decoration is enabled at the output group level. If you enable the feature in a given output group, all the outputs in that group have their manifests decorated.

To include manifest decoration in some outputs and not others, you must create two output groups of the specified type, for example, two HLS output groups.

Enabling Decoration – HLS

Manifest decoration is enabled at the output group level, which means that the manifests for all outputs in that group include instructions based on the SCTE-35 content.

1. In the channel that you are creating, make sure that you have set the ad avail mode. See [ERROR] BAD/MISSING LINK TEXT.

2. In the navigation pane, find the desired HLS output group.

3. In **Ad Marker**, choose **Add ad markers**.

4. For **HLS ad markers**, select the type of ad marker. For information about the different types of markers, see Sample Manifests - HLS.

5. Repeat to add more types of markers, as desired.

The manifest for each output will include a separate set of tags for each type that you select.

Enabling Decoration – Microsoft Smooth

With Microsoft Smooth, if you enable manifest decoration, instructions are inserted in the sparse track.

Manifest decoration is enabled at the output group level, which means that the sparse tracks for all outputs in that group will include instructions based on the SCTE-35 content.

The Procedure to Enable Decoration

1. In the channel that you are creating, make sure that you have set the ad avail mode. See [ERROR] BAD/MISSING LINK TEXT.

2. In the navigation pane, find the desired Microsoft Smooth output group.

3. For **Sparse track**, for **Sparse track type**, choose **SCTE_35**.

4. Complete **Acquisition point ID**, only if encryption is enabled on the output. Enter the address of the certificate.

How SCTE-35 Events Are Handled in Manifests and Sparse Tracks

When manifest decoration or sparse track is enabled, AWS Elemental MediaLive inserts up to three types of information. The triggers for inserting this information depend on the mode.

Types of Information

Type of Instruction	When Inserted
Base64	Information about all SCTE-35 messages in the output is incorporated into the manifest; the entire SCTE-35 message is added in base64 format.
Cue-out, Cue-in	SCTE-35 messages that are ad avails result in the insertion of cue-out, cue-in instructions.
Blackout	Only applies to the SCTE-35 Enhanced ad marker style (for HLS output; see [ERROR] BAD/MISSING LINK TEXT). SCTE-35 messages that are *not *ad avails result in the insertion of blackout start/end instructions, assuming that blackout is enabled. If blackout is not enabled, these instructions are not inserted.

Splice Insert Mode

Message Type ID: Splice Insert

Segmentation Type ID	Base64	Cue-out, Cue-in	Blackout
No segmentation descriptor present	Yes	Yes	
Provider advertisement	Yes	Yes	
Distributor advertisement	Yes	Yes	
Placement opportunity	Yes	Yes	
Other: Programs, Chapters, Network, Unscheduled	Yes		Yes

Message Type ID: Time Signal

Segmentation Type ID	Base64	Cue-out, Cue-in	Blackout
Provider advertisement	Yes	Yes	
Distributor advertisement	Yes	Yes	
Placement opportunity	Yes	Yes	

Segmentation Type ID	Base64	Cue-out, Cue-in	Blackout
Other: Programs, Chapters, Network, Unscheduled	Yes		Yes

For example, read the first line in the first table as follows: When a splice insert (with no segmentation descriptor) is encountered, the base64 and cue-out, cue-in information will be inserted in the manifest; blackout information will not be inserted.

Timesignal APOS Mode

Message Type ID: Splice Insert

Segmentation Type ID	Base64	Cue-out, Cue-in	Blackout
No segmentation descriptor present	Yes		
Provider advertisement	Yes		
Distributor advertisement	Yes		
Placement opportunity	Yes		
Other: Programs, Chapters, Network, Unscheduled	Yes		

Message Type ID: Time Signal

Segmentation Type ID	Base64	Cue-out, Cue-in	Blackout
Provider advertisement	Yes		
Distributor advertisement	Yes		
Placement opportunity	Yes	Yes	
Other: Programs, Chapters, Network, Unscheduled	Yes		Yes

For example, read the first line in the first table as follows: When a splice insert (with no segmentation descriptor) is encountered, the base64 information will be inserted in the manifest, and cue-out, cue-in information and blackout information will not be inserted.

Enabling Ad Avail Blanking

You can enable ad avail blanking to blank out the content for an SCTE-35 message that is considered an ad avail (as defined by the ad avail mode in Getting Ready: Set the Ad Avail Mode).

A similar feature is blackout.

Blanking involves the following processing:

- Replace the video content associated with this event with an image that you specify or is with a black image.
- Remove the audio that is associated with this event.
- Remove the captions that are associated with this event.

Comparison to Manifest Decoration and Passthrough

Ad avail blanking applies to all outputs. You cannot choose to blank out for some outputs (for example, the HLS output) and not blank out for others (for example, the Microsoft Smooth output). It is an all-or-nothing decision.

Manifest decoration and passthrough have a smaller scope: they apply only to outputs that support these features.

Take important note of this fact, because if you do *not* do passthrough and do *not* do manifest decoration in a given output (because they are not supported or because you choose not to) but you do implement blanking, there will be no markers for where the blanked content occurs. The only way to identify where this blanking is occurring will be to look for the IDR i-frames that identify where the SCTE-35 message used to be.

The Procedure to Enable Blanking

1. In the channel that you are creating, in the navigation pane, choose **General settings**.

2. In **Avail configuration**, set **Avail settings**, if you have not already done so:

   - SCTE-35 splice insert (default): Select this mode if the input uses splice inserts to indicate ad avails. The input might also contain messages for others events such as chapters or programs.

   - SCTE-35 time signal APOS: Select this mode if the input contains time signals of segmentation type **Placement opportunity**. The input might also contain messages for other events such as chapters or programs.

   The mode identifies which of all possible events are treated as triggers for ad avails and as triggers for blackouts. In turn, these triggers affect how manifests are decorated, when video is blanked, and when video is blacked out.

3. For **Ad avail offset**, set a value, if desired. See the help for this field.

4. In **web_delivery_allowed_flag** and **no_regional_blackout_flag**, choose appropriate values. For information about these fields, see [ERROR] BAD/MISSING LINK TEXT.

   - Follow (default): Observe the restriction and blank the content for the ad avail event.

   - Ignore: Ignore the restriction and do *not* blank the content for the ad avail event. **Warning** Never set both fields to Ignore.

   In **Avail blanking**, in **State**, choose **Enabled**.

5. In **Avail blanking image**, choose the appropriate value:

   - Disable: To use a plain black image for blanking.

   - Avail blanking image: To use a special image for blanking. In the **URI** field, type the path to a file in an S3 bucket. The file must be of type .bmp or .png. Also enter the user name and EC2 password key for accessing the S3 bucket. See [ERROR] BAD/MISSING LINK TEXT.

Triggers for Ad Avail Blanking

For ad avail blanking, the ad avail mode that you set controls which SCTE-35 events result in the blanking of the content.

Triggers in Splice Insert Mode

This section describes which message type and segmentation type combination is blanked by ad avail blanking when the Ad Avail mode is Splice Insert mode.

Message Type ID: Splice Insert

Segmentation Type ID	Blanked
No segmentation descriptor present	Yes
Provider advertisement	Yes
Distributor advertisement	Yes
Placement opportunity	Yes
Other: Programs, Chapters, Network, Unscheduled	No

Message Type ID: Time Signal

Segmentation Type ID	Blanked
Provider advertisement	Yes
Distributor advertisement	Yes
Placement opportunity	Yes
Other: Programs, Chapters, Network, Unscheduled	No

Triggers in Timesignal APOS Mode

This section describes which message type/segmentation type combination is blanked by ad avail blanking when the Ad Avail mode is Timesignal with APOS mode.

Message Type ID: Splice Insert

Segmentation Type ID	Blanked
No segmentation descriptor present	No
Provider advertisement	No
Distributor advertisement	No
Placement opportunity	No
Other: Programs, Chapters, Network, Unscheduled	No

Message Type ID: Time Signal

Segmentation Type ID	Blanked
Provider advertisement	No
Distributor advertisement	No

Segmentation Type ID	Blanked
Placement opportunity	Yes
Other: Programs, Chapters, Network, Unscheduled	No

Ad Avail Blanking Restriction Flags

Restrictions in the Input

SCTE-35 messages of type time_signal always contain segmentation descriptors.

SCTE-35 messages of type splice_insert might or might not include segmentation descriptors.

If the input has SCTE-35 messages that do include segmentation descriptors, these segmentation descriptors always include two types of flags. Each flag has a value of "true" or "false" and provides additional information as guidance for blanking in specific situations:

- web_delivery_allowed_flag

  - True means that there is no restriction on including the ad avail event's content in a stream that is intended for web delivery: there is no need to blank out content in streams intended for web delivery.

  - False means there is a restriction: the content should be blanked out.

- no_regional_blackout_flag

  (The wording of this flag is confusing. Think of it as the "regional_delivery_allowed_flag".)

  - True means that there is no restriction on including the ad avail event's video in a stream that is intended for regional markets: there is no need to blank out content in streams intended for regional markets.

  - False means there is a restriction: the content should be blanked out.

If neither flag is present (usually the case with splice_inserts), then both are considered to be false. Blanking should occur.

If both flags are present (which is usually the case; it is unusual to have only one flag present), then a "false" for one flag takes precedence over a "true" for the other flag. Blanking should occur.

Typically, in any given message in the input only one of these flags is ever set to false, so only one restriction is ever in place. There would typically never be *both* a regional delivery restriction and a web delivery restriction. This is because if content is considered restricted for regional delivery, then it would not also be considered restricted for web delivery (where the concept of a region makes no sense).

To summarize, this is the blanking logic that applies to each ad avail event that is encountered.

Blanking Logic for Ad Avail Events

	Content of corresponding SCTE-35 message: Web delivery allowed?	Content of corresponding SCTE-35 message: Regional delivery allowed?	Result	Comment
S1	Flag is not present	Flag is not present	Blanking occurs	This combination can only occur in a message type splice_insert (where the segmentation descriptor is optional).
S2	Flag is set to "true"	Flag is set to "true"	Blanking doesn't occur	
S3	Flag is set to "true"	Flag is set to "false"	Blanking occurs	

	Content of corresponding SCTE-35 message: Web delivery allowed?	Content of corresponding SCTE-35 message: Regional delivery allowed?	Result	Comment
S4	Flag is set to "false"	Flag is set to "true"	Blanking occurs	

AWS Elemental MediaLive Handling of Restrictions

You can modify this default blanking behavior by instructing AWS Elemental MediaLive to ignore a restriction flag that is set to false, so that blanking *not *occur for this ad avail event. In other words, to use this logic, "Even if the message indicates to blank content because a regional blackout is in place, do not follow this instruction. Ignore the fact that a regional blackout is in place and do not blank content".

You modify the behavior by setting fields in the channel. See [ERROR] BAD/MISSING LINK TEXT.

Restriction Flags with "Splice Insert"

If you select **Splice Insert** as the **Ad Avail** mode, then there is an assumption that the SCTE-35 ad avail message does *not* include the two restriction flags that are described earlier in this section. There is an assumption that every SCTE-35 ad avail message should result in an ad avail.

Therefore, if you know that the input contains splice inserts (not time signals), you should leave both restriction fields unchecked.

Enabling Blackout

You can enable blackout to blank out the content for an SCTE-35 message that is of type "other event" (as defined by the mode in Getting Ready: Set the Ad Avail Mode). For example, chapters and programs.

(A similar feature is described in [ERROR] BAD/MISSING LINK TEXT.)

Blackout involves the following processing:

- Replace the video content associated with the event with an image that you specify or is with a black image.
- Remove the audio that is associated with the event.
- Remove the captions that are associated with the event.

Comparison to Manifest Decoration and Passthrough

Blackout applies to all outputs. You cannot choose to black out for some outputs (for example, the HLS output) and not black out for others (for example, the Microsoft Smooth output). It is an all-or-nothing decision.

Manifest decoration and passthrough have a smaller scope: they apply only to outputs that support these features.

Take important note of this fact, because if you do *not* do passthrough and do *not* do manifest decoration in a given output (because they are not supported or because you choose not to) but you do implement blanking, there will be no "markers" for where the blanked content occurs. The only way of identifying where this blanking is occurring will be to look for the IDR i-frames that identify where the SCTE-35 message used to be.

The Procedure to Black out

1. In the channel that you are creating, in the navigation pane, choose **General settings**.

2. For **Avail configuration**, set **Avail settings**, if you have not already done so:

   - SCTE-35 splice insert (default): Select this mode if the input uses splice inserts to indicate ad avails. The input might also contain messages for others events such as chapters or programs.

   - SCTE-35 time signal APOS: Select this mode if the input contains time signals of segmentation type **Placement opportunity**. The input might also contain messages for other events such as chapters or programs.

     The mode identifies which of all possible events are treated as triggers for "ad avails" and as triggers for "blackouts." In turn, these triggers affect how manifests are decorated, when video is blanked, and when video is blacked out.

3. For **Ad avail offset**, set a value, if desired. See the help for this field.

4. For **web_delivery_allowed_flag** and **no_regional_blackout_flag**, choose appropriate values. For information about these fields, see [ERROR] BAD/MISSING LINK TEXT.

   - **Follow **(default): Observe the restriction and blank the content for the ad avail event.

   - **Ignore**: Ignore the restriction and do *not* blank the content for the ad avail event. **Warning** Never set both fields to **Ignore**.

5. In **Blackout slate**, in **State**, choose **Enabled**.

6. For **Blackout slate image**, choose the appropriate value:

   - **Disable**: To use a plain black image for blackout.

   - **Avail blanking image**: To use a special image for blackout. In the **URI** field, enter the path to a file in an Amazon S3 bucket. The file must be of type .bmp or .png. Also enter the user name and EC2 password key for accessing the S3 bucket. For information on this key, see [ERROR] BAD/MISSING LINK TEXT.

7. If you want to enable network end blackout (in other words, black out content when network transmission has ended and remove blackout only when network transmission resumes), continue reading. If you don't want to enable it, you have now finished setting up.

8. For **Network end blackout**, choose **Enabled**.

9. For **Network end blackout image**, choose the appropriate value:

   - **Disable**: To use a plain black image for blackout.

   - **Network end blackout image**: To use a special image for network end blackout. In the **URI** field, enter the path to a file in an Amazon S3 bucket. The file must be of type .bmp or .png. Also enter the user name and EC2 password key for accessing the S3 bucket. See [ERROR] BAD/MISSING LINK TEXT.

10. For **Additional settings**, in **Network ID**, type the EIDR ID of the network in the format 10.nnnn/xxxx-xxxx- xxxx- xxxx-xxxx-c (case insensitive). Only network end events with this ID will trigger blackout.

Triggers for Blackout

The blackout feature is triggered only by time_signal messages of segmentation type **Other**. It is not triggered by splice_insert messages of any segmentation type, and is not triggered by time_signal messages of any type except **Other**.

SCTE-35 messages of type ID "splice insert" and messages of type ID "time signal" can both include "Other" time_signal messages. Therefore, when enabling blackout, the ad avail mode is not relevant. Blackout works the same with either mode.

The segmentation ID triggers blackout based on "events," as shown in the following table.

SCTE-35 Segmentation Type	Blacked out
Chapter Start	Start blacking out
Chapter End	End blacking out
Network Start	End blacking out
Network End	Start blacking out
Program Start	Start blacking out
Program End	End blacking out
Unscheduled Event Start	Start blacking out
Unscheduled Event End	End blacking out

For example, if the blackout feature is enabled, then blanking always occurs when a Program Start message is encountered and always ends when a Program End message is encountered.

Note that the triggers for blackout on a Network event are different from the other events:

- With Network, blanking starts when the Network *End* instruction is encountered.

- With other events, blanking starts when the "Event *Start*" instruction is encountered.

End Event Trigger Hierarchy

Events have the following "strength hierarchy."

SCTE-35 Segmentation Type	Strength
Network	1 (Strongest)
Unscheduled Event	2
Program	3
Chapter	4 (Weakest)

A blackout can be ended only by an event of equal or greater strength than the event that started it.

For example, if the blackout is started by a Program Start, it can be ended by a Network Start, an Unscheduled Event End or a Program End. It cannot be ended by a Chapter End. AWS Elemental MediaLive ignores the "end blackout" instruction implied by the Chapter End.

Blackout Restriction Flags

Restrictions in the Input

The segmentation descriptors in messages that are blackout triggers always include two types of flags. These flags provide additional information as guidance for blackout in specific situations:

- web_delivery_allowed_flag

  - True means that there is no restriction on including the event's content in a stream that is intended for web delivery. There is no need to black out content in streams intended for web delivery.

  - False means that there is a restriction. The content should be blacked out.

- no_regional_blackout_flag

  - True means that there is no restriction on including the event's video in a stream intended for regional markets. There is no need to black out content in streams intended for regional markets.

  - False means that there is a restriction. The content should be blacked out.

If both flags are present (which is usually the case; it is unusual to have only one flag present), then a "false" for one flag takes precedence over a "true" for the other flag. Blackout should occur.

Typically, in any given message in the input only one of these flags is ever set to false, so only one restriction is ever in place. There would typically never be both a regional delivery restriction and a web delivery restriction. This is because if content is considered restricted for regional delivery, then it would not also be considered restricted for web delivery (where the concept of a region makes no sense).

To summarize, this is the blackout logic that applies to each event that is encountered.

	Content of corresponding SCTE-35 message: Web delivery allowed?	Content of corresponding SCTE-35 message: Regional delivery allowed?	Result	Comment
S1	Flag is not present	Flag is not present	Blackout occurs	Never occurs in messages that are blackout triggers
S2	Flag is set to "true"	Flag is set to "true"	Blackout doesn't occur	
S3	Flag is set to "true"	Flag is set to "false"	Blackout occurs	
S4	Flag is set to "false"	Flag is set to "true"	Blackout occurs	

AWS Elemental MediaLive Handling of Restrictions

You can modify this default blackout behavior by instructing AWS Elemental MediaLive to ignore a restriction flag that is set to false, so that blackout will *not *occur for this event. In other words, to use this logic, ""Even if the message indicates to black out content because a regional blackout is in place, do not follow this instruction. Ignore the fact that a regional blackout is in place and do not black out content".

You modify the behavior by setting fields in the channel.

SCTE-35 Passthrough or Removal

You can set up the AWS Elemental MediaLive channel so that SCTE-35 messages from the input is passed through (included) in the data stream for the following outputs:

- Outputs in an Archive output group.
- Outputs in an HLS output group.
- Outputs in a UDP output group.

Alignment with Video
The PTS of the SCTE-35 message is adjusted to match the PTS of the corresponding video frame.

Passthrough Is at the Output Level
SCTE-35 passthrough or removal applies at the output level. The messages are passed through or removed only in a specific output. The default behavior (if you do not change the configuration fields) is to remove the messages.

The Procedure for Archive

1. In the channel that you are creating, find the **Archive** output group that contains the output that you want to set up.

2. Choose that output.

3. In **PID settings**, complete the following fields:

   - **SCTE-35 control**: Set to **Passthrough**.
   - **SCTE-35 PID**: Leave the default PID or enter the PID where you want the SCTE-35 messages to go.

4. If appropriate, repeat for other outputs in this or other **Archive** output groups.

All SCTE-35 messages from the input are included in the data stream of the outputs that you have set up.

The Procedure for HLS

1. In the channel that you are creating, find the HLS output group that contains the output that you want to set up.

2. Choose that output.

3. In **PID settings**, complete the following fields:

   - **SCTE-35 behavior**: Set to **Passthrough**.
   - **SCTE-35 PID**: Leave the default PID or enter the PID where you want the SCTE-35 messages to go.

4. If appropriate, repeat for other outputs in this or other HLS output groups.

All SCTE-35 messages from the input will be included in the data stream of the outputs that you have set up.

The Procedure for UDP

1. In the channel that you are creating, find the UDP output group that contains the output that you want to set up.

2. Choose that output.

3. In **PID settings**, complete the following fields:

   - **SCTE-35 control**: Set to **Passthrough**.
   - **SCTE-35 PID**: Leave the default PID or enter the PID where you want the SCTE-35 messages to go.

4. If appropriate, repeat for other outputs in this or other UDP output groups.

All SCTE-35 messages from the input will be included in the data stream of the outputs that you have set up.

Sample Manifests - HLS

AWS Elemental MediaLive supports the following HLS manifest styles:

- Adobe
- Elemental
- SCTE-35 Enhanced

This section describes the ad marker tagging for each style.

Ad Marker: Adobe

Inserts a CUE: DURATION for each ad avail. Does not insert any CUE-OUT CONT (continuation tags) to indicate to a player joining midbreak that there is a current avail. This does not insert a CUE-IN tag at the end of the avail.

Structure
[See the AWS documentation website for more details]

Tag Contents

- CUE:DURATION contains the following:
    - duration – Duration in fractional seconds
    - id – An identifier, unique among all ad avails CUE tags
    - type – SpliceOut
    - time – The PTS time for the ad avail, in fractional seconds

Example
This is the tag for an ad avail lasting 414.171 PTS:

```
1  #EXT-X-CUE:DURATION="201.467",ID="0",TYPE="SpliceOut",TIME="414.171"
```

Ad Marker: Elemental

Structure

[See the AWS documentation website for more details]

Tag Contents

- CUE-OUT contains DURATION
- CUE-OUT-CONT contains Elapsed time and Duration
- CUE-IN has no content

Example

```
1  #EXT-X-CUE-OUT:30.000
2  .
3  .
4  .
5  # EXT-X-CUE-OUT-CONT: 8.308/30
6  .
```

```
 7 .
 8 .
 9 # EXT-X-CUE-OUT-CONT: 20.391/30
10 .
11 .
12 .
13 # EXT-X-CUE-IN
```

Ad Marker: SCTE-35 Enhanced

Structure

[See the AWS documentation website for more details]

Tag Contents

- OATCLS-SCTE35 containing the base64 encoded raw bytes of the original SCTE-35 ad avail message.
- ASSET containing the CAID or UPID as specified in the original SCTE35 message.
- 1 CUE-OUT per ad avail.
- CUE-OUT-CONT containing the following:
  - The elapsed time of the avail.
  - The duration declared in the original SCTE35 message.
  - SCTE35 containing the base64 encoded raw bytes of the original SCTE-35 ad avail message.
    These lines repeat until the ad avail ends.
- CUE-IN to indicate the end of the avail.

Example

```
 1 #EXT-OATCLS-SCTE35:/DA0AAAAAAAAAAAABQb+ADAQ6QAeAhxDVUVJQAAA03/PAAEUrEoICAAAAAg+2UBNAAANvrtoQ==
 2 #EXT-X-ASSET:CAID=0x0000000020FB6501
 3 #EXT-X-CUE-OUT:201.467
 4 .
 5 .
 6 .
 7 #EXT-X-CUE-OUT-CONT:ElapsedTime=5.939,Duration=201.467,SCTE35=/DA0AAAA...+AAg+2UBNAAANvrtoQ==
 8 .
 9 .
10 .
11 #EXT-X-CUE-IN
```

Starting and Stopping a Channel

- Starting a Channel
- Stopping a Channel

Starting a Channel

1. Open the AWS Elemental MediaLive console at https://console\.aws\.amazon\.com/medialive?region="region"\.

2. In the navigation pane, choose **Channels**.

3. On the **Channels** page, choose the channel that you want to start.

4. Choose **Start**. The channel state changes to one of the following:

   - **Starting**

   - **Recovering** (indicates that encoding has started on one of the destinations but not the other)

   - **Running** (encoding on both destinations)

5. Choose the channel name. The details for the channel appear. The content pane shows these sections:

Stopping a Channel

You can stop a channel that is running.

1. Choose the channel.

2. Choose **Stop**.

Handling AWS Elemental MediaLive Alerts

AWS Elemental MediaLive provides feedback to you on the status of channels. It does this by creating Amazon CloudWatch events that hold alert information. You can manage these events using Amazon CloudWatch event rules and deliver them in emails or SMS messages. You can deliver events to a number of destinations; this chapter describes how to deliver them via the Amazon Simple Notification Service (SNS).

For complete information about the options for managing events using Amazon CloudWatch, see the Cloudwatch User Guide.

For complete information about using SNS, see the SNS Developer Guide.

Option 1: Send all AWS Elemental MediaLive Events to an Email Address

This option shows how to set up is to send all events to a single email address. The drawback of this setup is that the email account will receive a large volume of emails. Therefore this setup is not recommended in a production environment.

You must perform this setup in each region where channels are running.

Step 1: Create a Subscription

You create a subscription to set up a specific email address so that it automatically receives email notifications when any event occurs in AWS Elemental MediaLive. You need to identify an email recipient for the emails.

We illustrate this procedure with the example of setting up to send emails with the sender appearing as "MediaLive" and the subject line as "MediaLive_alert".

1. Sign in to the AWS Management Console and open the Amazon Simple Notification Service console.

2. In the navigation panel, choose **SNS dashboard**, then choose **Topics**.

3. On the **SNS dashboard** page, choose **Create new topic**.

4. In **Topic** name, type the name you want for the subject of the email. For example, "MediaLive_alert".

5. In Display name type the name you want for the sender of the email. For example "MediaLive".

6. Choose **Create topic**.

7. SNS creates the topic and displays the ARN in the **Topic details** panel. For example, arn:aws:sns:us-west-2:111122223333:MediaLive, where 111122223333 is your AWS account.

8. Copy this ARN to your clipboard.

9. In the navigation panel, choose **Subscriptions**.

10. In the **Subscriptions** page, choose **Create subscriptions**.

11. In the **Create subscriptions** pane, in **Topic ARN**, type or paste the ARN.

12. In **Protocol**, choose **Email**.

13. In **Email address**, type the email address of the recipient. You must be able to log onto this email account because you will be sending a confirmation email to this address.

14. Choose **Create subscription**.

    SNS sends a confirmation email to the address you specified.

15. Log onto that email account and display the email. Choose the Confirm subscription link in the email to enable the subscription. A confirmation window appears in a web browser. You can close this window.

Step 2: Create a CloudWatch Rule

You now create a rule that says "When CloudWatch receives any event from aws.medialive, invoke the specified SNS topic – in other words, send an email to the subscribed email address.

1. Sign in to the AWS Management Console and open the Amazon CloudWatch console.

2. On the navigation pane, choose **Events**.

3. In **Welcome to CloudWatch Events**, choose **Create Rule**.

4. In** Step 1**, in **Event Source**, choose **Event Pattern**.

5. Change **Build event pattern to match** to **Custom event pattern**.

6. In the entry box, type the following:

```
1  {
2    "source": [
3      "aws.medialive"
4    ]
5  }
```

7. From the right-hand panel, choose **Add target**.

8. Choose **SNS topic**.

9. In **Topic**, choose the topic you created, for example, "MediaLive_alert".

10. Choose **Configure details**

11. In **Configure input**, choose **Matched event**.

12. Type a name and optional description, then choose **Create rule**.

Now, whenever an alert occurs in AWS Elemental MediaLive, an event will be sent to Amazon CloudWatch. This event will trigger the rule that instructs CloudWatch to send an email to the email address specified in the SNS subscription.

Option 2: Send Events for Specific Channels to an Email Address

You can set up to send all events for a specific channel (or channels) to one email. You must perform this setup in each region where channels are running.

Create as many subscriptions and rules combinations as required. Follow the steps for Option 1, with these differences:

- When creating the SNS subscription, you may want to fine-tune the topic, for example "MediaLive_notifications_channel_1234567".

- When creating the CloudWatch rule, you create a rule with an event pattern that identifies aws.medialive as the "event source" and the ARN for the specific channel as "the resource" within that event source, as follows:

```
1 {""
2   source: ["
3     aws."medialive
4   ]""
5   resources: ["
6     arn:aws:medialive:us-west-2:111122223333:channel":1234567
7   ]
8 }
```

The resource is the ARN for the desired channel. You can obtain this ARN from the channels list in the AWS Elemental MediaLive console.

This rule that says "When CloudWatch receives any event from aws.medialive for channel 1234567, invoke the specified SNS topic – in other words, send an email to the subscribed email address."

If desired, you can enter more than one channel in the resources section. For example:

```
1 ""
2   resources: ["
3     arn:aws:medialive:us-west-2:111122223333:channel":1234567,"
4     arn:aws:medialive:us-west-2:111122223333:channel":2223334
5   ]
```

Reference: Supported Captions

This section contains tables that specify the codecs that are supported in inputs and the codecs that are supported in outputs.

There are several factors that control your ability to output captions in a given format:

- The type of input container. A given input container can contain captions in some formats and not in others.

- The format of the input captions. A given format of captions can be converted to some formats and not to others.

- The type of output containers. A given output container supports some caption formats and not others.

- How to Read the Supported Captions Information

- General Information on Supported Formats

- Formats Supported in an HLS Output

- Formats Supported in an MPEG2-TS File Output or MPEG2-UDP Streaming Output

- Formats Supported in a Microsoft Smooth Output

How to Read the Supported Captions Information

To determine if the input container and input captions that you have received are capable of producing the desired output captions, consult the tables in the following sections and follow these steps:

1. Find the table for your output container.

2. In that table, find the container type of the input you have been provided with and then find the input captions that are in that container.

3. In the third column, look for the output caption format you require.

   If the format is listed, then your input is suitable.

   If the format is not listed, you must ask the provider of that input to provide an input container that includes input captions that can be converted to the required output format.

General Information on Supported Formats

The following table shows the supported formats, specifies whether they are supported in inputs or outputs, and specifies the standard that defines each format.

Caption	Supported in Input	Supported in Output	Description
Ancillary data	Yes		From MXF input, data that is compliant with "SMPTE 291M: Ancillary Data Package and Space Formatting" and that is contained in ancillary data.
ARIB	Yes	Yes	Captions that are compliant with ARIB STD-B37 Version 2.4.
Burn-in	N/A	Yes	From input: It is technically impossible for the encoder to read burn-in captions. Therefore, from an input viewpoint, they cannot be considered to be captions.For output: Burn-in captions are captions that are converted into text and then overlaid on top of the picture directly in the video stream.
DVB-Sub	Yes	Yes	Captions that are compliant with ETSI EN 300 743.
Embedded	Yes	Yes	Captions that are compliant with the EIA-608 standard (also known as CEA-608 or SMPTE-259M or "line 21 captions") or the CEA-708 standard (also known as EIA-708).
Embedded+SCTE-20	Yes	Yes	Captions that have both embedded and SCTE-20 in the video. The embedded captions are inserted before the SCTE-20 captions.

Caption	Supported in Input	Supported in Output	Description
SCTE-20	Yes		Captions that are compliant with the standard "SCTE 20 2012 Methods for Carriage of CEA-608 Closed Captions and Non-Real Time Sampled Video."
SCTE-20+Embedded		Yes	Captions that are compliant with SCTE-43. The SCTE-20 captions are inserted in the video before the embedded captions.
SCTE-27	Yes	Yes	Captions that are compliant with the standard "SCTE-27 (2011), Subtitling Methods for Broadcast Cable."
Teletext	Yes	Yes	From TS input: Captions in the EBU Teletext format.
TTML	Yes	Yes	Captions files that are compliant with the standard "Timed Text Markup Language 1 (TTML1) (Second Edition)."
WebVTT		Yes	Captions that are compliant with "webvtt: The Web Video Text Tracks Format" (http://dev.w3.org/html5/webvtt/).

Formats Supported in an HLS Output

Find the table for your output container, then within the table, look up your input container and captions type. The supported caption formats are listed in the last column.

Source Caption Container	Source Caption Input	Supported Output Captions
HLS Container	Embedded	Burn-inEmbeddedWeb-VTT
	SCTE-20	Burn-inEmbeddedWeb-VTT
RTMP Container	Embedded	Burn-inEmbeddedWeb-VTT
MPEG2-TS Container	Embedded	Burn-inEmbeddedWeb-VTT
	SCTE-20	Burn-inEmbeddedWeb-VTT
	Teletext	Burn-inWeb-VTT
	ARIB	None
	DVB-Sub	Burn-in
	SCTE-27	Burn-in

Formats Supported in an MPEG2-TS File Output or MPEG2-UDP Streaming Output

Find the table for your output container, then within the table, look up your input container and captions type. The supported caption formats are listed in the last column.

Source Caption Container	Source Caption Input	Supported Output Captions
HLS Container	Embedded	Burn-inDVB-SubEmbeddedEmbedded+SCTE-20SCTE-20+Embedded
	SCTE-20	Burn-inDVB-SubEmbeddedEmbedded+SCTE-20SCTE-20+Embedded
RTMP Container	Embedded	Burn-inDVB-SubEmbeddedEmbedded+SCTE-20SCTE-20+Embedded
MPEG2-TS Container	Embedded	Burn-inDVB-SubEmbeddedEmbedded+SCTE-20SCTE-20+Embedded
	SCTE-20	Burn-inDVB-SubEmbeddedEmbedded+SCTE-20SCTE-20+Embedded
	Teletext	Burn-inDVB-SubTeletext
	ARIB	ARIB
	DVB-Sub	Burn-inDVB-Sub
	SCTE-27	Burn-inDVB-SubSCTE-27

Formats Supported in a Microsoft Smooth Output

Find the table for your output container, then within the table, look up your input container and captions type. The supported caption formats are listed in the last column.

Source Caption Container	Source Caption Input	Supported Output Captions
HLS Container	Embedded	Burn-inTTML
	SCTE-20	Burn-inTTML
RTMP Container	Embedded	Burn-inTTML
MPEG2-TS Container	Embedded	Burn-inTTML
	SCTE-20	Burn-inTTML
	Teletext	Burn-inTTML
	ARIB	None
	DVB-Sub	
	SCTE-27	

Reference: Supported Containers and Codecs

- Supported Input Types
- Supported Codecs for Inputs
- Supported Codecs for Outputs

Supported Input Types

AWS Elemental MediaLive supports the following input sources.

AWS Elemental MediaLive Option (on the Create Input page)	Use Case	Protocol	URI Format	Stream Input Supported	File Input Supported
RTP	Push a stream to a fixed endpoint on AWS Elemental MediaLive, using the RTP protocol.	RTP	rtp://:5000/	Yes	
RTMP Pull	Pull a stream from an external endpoint using the RTMP protocol.	RTMP Pull	rtmp://:1935/	Yes	
RTMP Push	Push a stream to a fixed endpoint on AWS Elemental MediaLive, using the RTMP protocol. For the application name, only "live" is supported.	RTMP Push	/	Yes	
HLS	Pull an HLS stream or file from an external endpoint using the HTTP protocol.	HTTP	The path to the M3U8 manifest: http://[:port]/pa file.m3u8	Yes	Yes
HLS	Pull an HLS stream or file from an external endpoint using the HTTPS protocol.	HTTPS	The path to the M3U8 manifest: https:///-path/file.m3u8	Yes	Yes
HLS	Pull an HLS stream or file from an Amazon S3 bucket.	Amazon S3	The path to the M3U8 manifest: s3:///-path/file.m3u8	Yes	Yes

AWS Elemental MediaLive Option (on the Create Input page)	Use Case	Protocol	URI Format	Stream Input Supported	File Input Supported
HLS	Pull an HLS stream or file from an Amazon S3 bucket, using a secure connection.	HTTPS	The path to the M3U8 manifest: s3ssl:///-path/file.m3u8	Yes	Yes
HLS	Pull an HLS stream or file from an AWS Elemental MediaStore container, using a secure connection.	HTTPS	The path to the M3U8 manifest: mediastoressl://eri39n.ediastore.us-west-2.amazon-aws.com/premium/canada/m-law.m3u8	Yes	Yes

Ways of Ingesting: Push and Pull

- A push input works as follows: the source attempts to deliver to an endpoint that is specified in the AWS Elemental MediaLive input. In the case of RTP protocols, the source is unaware of whether the content is being ingested by the AWS Elemental MediaLive channel. In the case of RTMP, there must be a handshake between the source and the AWS Elemental MediaLive channel so that the source will have knowledge of the status of the input.

  When the channel (that is connected to this input) is started, AWS Elemental MediaLive reacts to the source (RTP) or responds to the handshake message (RTMP) and ingests it. When the channel is not running, AWS Elemental MediaLive does not react; the source continues to publish to the endpoint (RTP) or goes into a paused state (RTMP), but AWS Elemental MediaLive does not pay attention.

  A push input works only with a streaming source.

- A pull input works as follows: the source continually publishes to an endpoint that is outside of AWS Elemental MediaLive. When the channel (that is connected to the input) is running, AWS Elemental MediaLive connects to the input and ingests the content.

When the channel is not running, AWS Elemental MediaLive does not connect to the input. (There might be other applications that do connect.)

A pull input works with a streaming input (where the source is continually being published) or a file input (where the source is put on the endpoint and then does not change until the next time it is put).

Supported Codecs for Inputs

Container	Video Codecs	Audio Codecs
RTP (MPEG TS)	H.264 (AVC), HEVC (H.265), MPEG-2	AAC, Dolby Digital, Dolby Digital Plus, MPEG Audio, PCM
HLS	H.264 (AVC)	AAC, Dolby Digital, Dolby Digital Plus
RTMP	H.264 (AVC)	AAC

Supported Codecs for Outputs

Supported Codecs for File Outputs

Container	Video Codecs	Audio Codecs
MPEG-2 TS	H.264 (AVC)	AAC, Dolby Digital, Dolby Digital Plus, MPEG-1 Layer II
HLS	H.264 (AVC)	AAC, Dolby Digital, Dolby Digital Plus
Microsoft Smooth	H.264 (AVC)	AAC, Dolby Digital, Dolby Digital Plus

Streaming Outputs for Streaming Outputs

Container	Video Codecs	Audio Codecs
UDP	H.264 (AVC)	AAC, Dolby Digital, Dolby Digital Plus
HLS	H.264 (AVC)	AAC, Dolby Digital, Dolby Digital Plus
Microsoft Smooth	H.264 (AVC)	AAC, Dolby Digital, Dolby Digital Plus

Reference: Identifiers for Variable Data

Identifiers for variable data are $ codes that you can include in a field value to represent variable data. Typically, the variable data (for example, d for the date) is resolved when you run the channel. You can include them in any of the fields that make up part of the output destination:

- Destination in Output group
- Name modifier in Output
- Segment modifier in Output

At runtime, the identifier is resolved to the appropriate data. For example, dt resolves to a date and time.

Be careful when using these identifiers to make sure that the channel does not end up with two (or more) outputs with identical destinations. If this were to happen, the channel would pass validation upon creation, but it would fail on start.

Identifier	Format	Description
dt	YYYYMMDDTHHMMSS	UTC date and time of the start time of the channel (for all outputs except HLS) or the date and time of each segment (for HLS outputs)
d	YYYYMMDD	UTC date of the start time of the channel (for all outputs except HLS) or the date and time of each segment (for HLS outputs)
t	HHMMSS	Start time of the channel (for all outputs except HLS) or the time of each segment (for HLS outputs)
rv	Kb	Video bitrate
ra	Kb	Total of all audio bitrates in the output.
rc	Kb	Container bitrate for the output, or the sum of video and all audio bitrates for the output, if container bitrate is not specified.
w	Pixels	Horizontal resolution
h	Pixels	Vertical resolution
f	Integer	FPS Framerate without decimal places. For example "23.976" appears as "23"
fn	Filename	Name of input file, excluding the extension ex Extension Extension of the output file
$$	$	Escaped $
%0n	Padding modifier	Modifier for any data identifier. The modifier pads the resolved value with leading zeros. Format is %0n, where n is a number. For example, to ensure the resolved value in the h identifier is 5 characters long, specify the identifier as $h%05$. If the vertical resolution is "720", then the resolved, padded value is "00720"

The rules for which identifiers can be used in a given destination field depend on the output type:

Field	Applicable Output Types	Acceptable Identifiers
Destination in Output group	Archive, HLS, Microsoft Smooth	dt, d, t, fn
Name modifier in Output	Archive, Microsoft Smooth	All except ra and rc
Name modifier in Output	HLS	All
Segment modifier in Output	Archive, Microsoft Smooth	All except ra and rc
Segment modifier in Output	HLS	All

Limits in AWS Elemental MediaLive

The following table describes limits in AWS Elemental MediaLive. For information about limits that can be changed, see AWS Service Limits.

Resource	Default Limit
Maximum inputs	5 (can request more)
Maximum input security groups	5 (can request more)
Maximum channels	5 (can request more)

Document History for User Guide

The following table describes the documentation for this release of AWS Elemental MediaLive.

- **API version: latest**
- **Latest documentation update:** November 27, 2017

Change	Description	Date
New service and guide	This is the initial release of AWS Elemental MediaLive User Guide.	November 27, 2017
Input specification feature	Input specification fields ensure that the service allocates sufficient processing resources and correctly calculates processing charges. See [ERROR] BAD/MISSING LINK TEXT.	February 15, 2018
Channel edit feature	Editing of the fields in an existing (saved) channel is now supported. See [ERROR] BAD/MISSING LINK TEXT.	February 15, 2018
Custom template feature	Users can create custom templates from existing channels, and can import those templates into new channels. See [ERROR] BAD/MISSING LINK TEXT.	February 15, 2018

Note

The AWS Media Services are not designed or intended for use with applications or in situations requiring fail-safe performance, such as life safety operations, navigation or communication systems, air traffic control, or life support machines in which the unavailability, interruption or failure of the services could lead to death, personal injury, property damage or environmental damage. A component of AWS Elemental MediaLive is licensed under the AVC patent portfolio license for the personal and non-commercial use of a consumer to (i) encode video in compliance with the AVC standard ("AVC video") and/or (ii) decode AVC video that was encoded by a consumer engaged in a personal and non-commercial activity and/or was obtained from a video provider licensed to provide AVC video. No license is granted or shall be implied for any other use. A component of AWS Elemental MediaLive is licensed under the mpeg-4 patent portfolio license for the personal and non-commercial use of a consumer for (i) encoding video in compliance with the mpeg-4 visual standard ("mpeg-4 video") and/or (ii) decoding mpeg-4 video that was encoded by a consumer engaged in a personal and non-commercial activity and/or was obtained from a video provider licensed to provide AVC video. No license is granted or shall be implied for any other use. Additional information may be obtained from MPEG-LA, LLC. See http://www.mpegla.com. AWS Elemental MediaLive may contain Dolby Digital and Dolby Digital Plus, which are protected under international and U.S. copyright laws as unpublished works. Dolby Digital and Dolby Digital Plus are confidential and proprietary to Dolby Laboratories. Their reproduction or disclosure, in whole or in part, or the production of derivative works therefrom without the express permission of Dolby Laboratories is prohibited. © Copyright 2003-2015 Dolby Laboratories. All rights reserved.

AWS Glossary

For the latest AWS terminology, see the AWS Glossary in the *AWS General Reference*.